Notes from the Publisher

Welcome to a glimpse into the world of internatio[...]or you to be able to explore beyond the boundaries of the coun[...]iber artists are doing.

In many countries, rather than learning from vario[...]ending years progressing from simple techniques to the extre[...]d sewing and quilting by hand is honored and as such, hand[...]

This book was written in its original language, Japa[...][...]ne our best to make the directions for each project easy to ur[...][...]e some level of quilting experience, while maintaining the appearance and intent of the original author and publisher.

We hope the beautifully designed handmade items in this book inspire and encourage you to make them for yourself.

- Important Tips Before You Begin -

The following facts might suggest that intermediate or advanced quilters will be more comfortable working on these projects.

- Techniques -

Beyond the foundational techniques and two Step-by-Step lessons, Ms. Saito does not go into detailed descriptions of specific quilting or sewing methods for each project. She assumes that the creator is familiar with sewing, quilting and bag-making techniques to some degree and thus relies heavily on the creator's ability to figure out the directions that are not specifically written out. It is advisable to read through and understand each project's direction page from beginning to end, including finding the corresponding patterns on the included pattern sheets before beginning.

- Measurements -

The original designs were created using the metric system for dimensions. In order to assist you, we have included the imperial system measurements in brackets. However, please note that samples that appear in the book were created and tested using the metric system. Thus, you will find that if you use the imperial measurements to make the projects, the items you make will not be exactly the same size as when using the metric measurements.

- Patterns/Templates -

Full pattern information for each project appears in several different ways: a) in the materials list b) in the illustrations and captions c) in the pattern sheet insert. One must read through all the instructions carefully to understand what size to cut the fabric and related materials, including instructions for each project relating to seam allowances.

- Notions/Accessories -

As this book is all about bags, each project will call for a variety of accessories such as zippers, handles, and hardware. While the originals were made with items from Japan, most if not all of the accessories seen have comparable items or are available around the world. However, some of the accessories are available through Yoko Saito's quilt shop in Japan. See the copyright page for further information.

Stitch Publications, 2014

GW01458840

Yoko Saito's
Bags for Everyday Use

Scandinavia, United Kingdom, France, Italy, United States of America

Stitch
PUBLICATIONS

Introduction

Over the years since I began quilting, I have been blessed to have been able to travel the world and visit many countries. Five regions or countries in particular have left a deep impression upon me: Scandinavia, the United Kingdom, France, Italy and the United States of America.

The unique patchwork quilts and handicrafts that I ran across reflect their cultures and geography and color my unforgettable memories of each country. I like to think that I was able to internalize just a little bit of what their everyday lives must be like, and with those thoughts designs began to form in my mind. I began by connecting colors, motifs and even architectural shapes that I attributed to each country. As I turned those ideas around in my mind, I decided that they lent themselves nicely to quilted bags. I wanted to design bags that were not only practical for everyday use, but also beautifully designed in form and function.

My wish is that you will find that one of these bags speaks to you as you make something beautiful and useful with your gifted hands.

Yoko Saito

Contents

SCANDINAVIA

Living in Scandinavia is to be surrounded by magnificent nature and clear blue skies. Craftsmanship is passed down through the generations. I can only hope that I was able to blend both the splendor of their nature and culture in these handbags.

1 Songbird Handbag

The motif of the bird was inspired by a necklace that I found on a trip to Sweden. Integrated with a floral design, the appliqué and embroidery along with the unusual shape make this bag unique.

Instructions - p. 74

4

2 Floral Appliqué Boston Bag

The soft taupe colors with an easy access pocket on the side make up this Boston bag. The appliqué fabrics and embroidery floss, all variations of white, lend it a feminine air.

Instructions - p. 76

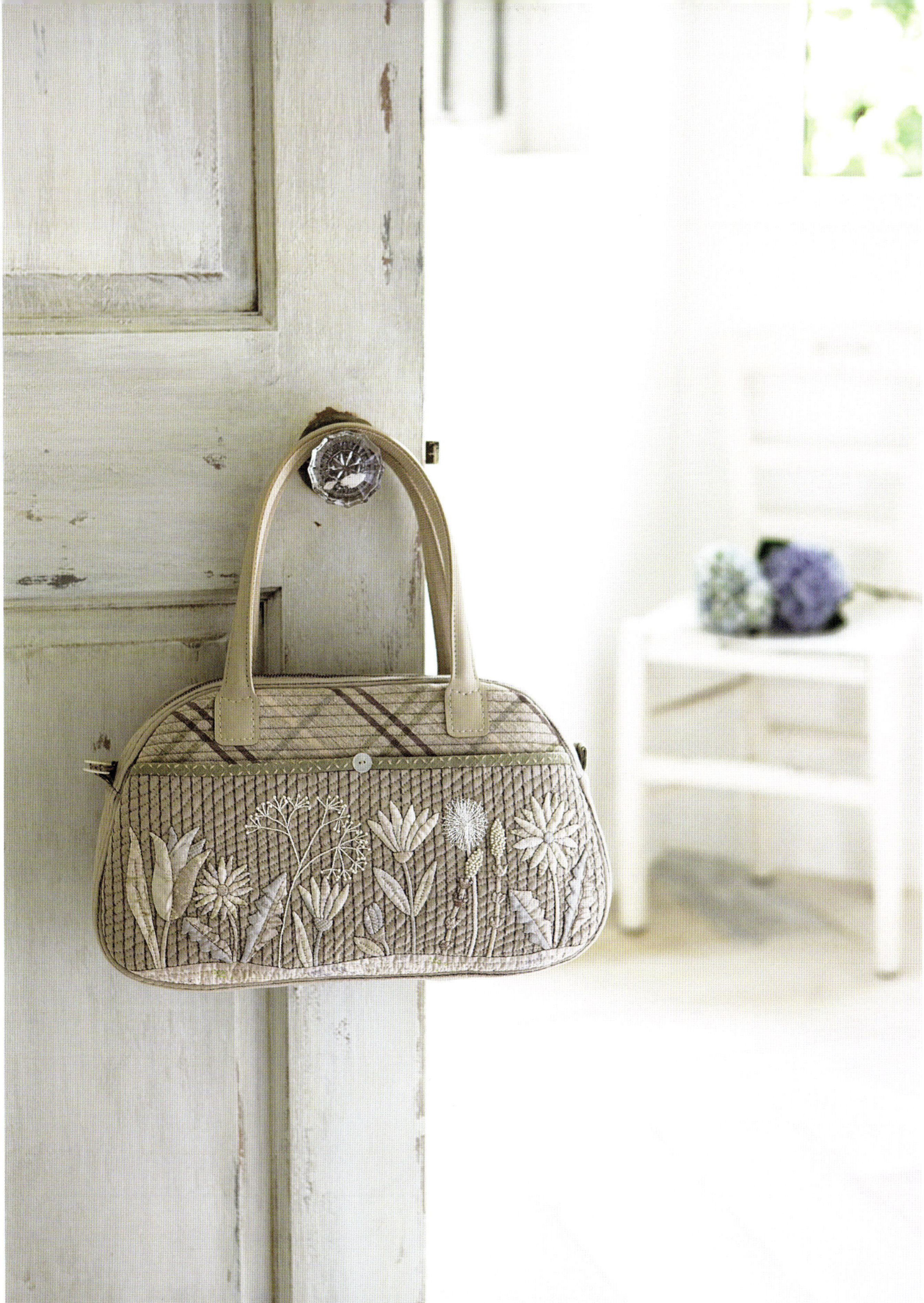

3 Appliquéd Bird Pouch

The warmth and joy of handwork come through in these appliqué motifs that hint at Scandinavian design in this little pouch.

Step-by-Step Instructions - p. 64

4 Branches & Berries Shoulder Bag

This simple, yet elegant design depicting images in nature is a highlight of this fashionable bag. A perfect size to fit a notebook; throw it over your shoulder and head out for the day.

Instructions - p. 78

5. Floral Star Handbag

This unique bag made up of trapezoids will come together beautifully if you sew the front, back and gussets together precisely by hand. I chose a color scheme with clarity for the appliqués to make them stand out. The leather handle and decorative zipper pull give the bag a certain elegance.

Instructions - p. 80

UNITED
KINGDOM

The United Kingdom is said to be the birthplace of patchwork and quilting. Single shapes sewn together, such as squares or hexagons, are often seen in the antique appliquéd quilts that can be found in museums that hint at the beginnings of traditional quilting designs.

6 Grandmother's Flower Garden Tote

Twenty-four blocks of eleven hexagons sewn together in Grandmother's Flower Garden pattern make up the body of this tote. Add a border to the opening along with an elliptical-shaped bottom for an original look.

Instructions - p. 82

14

7 Lovers Mini-Pouch with Handles

The stripes and checks remind me of classic British fabric. It's a convenient size whether you use it by itself or to hold things within a larger bag. Don't the figures remind you of a happy and carefree couple of days gone by?

Instructions - p. 84

8 Things We Love Bucket Bag

This one-handled bucket bag showcases a lady on one side, a gentleman on the other, each surrounded by different appliquéd animals and objects.

Instructions - p. 86

9 Around the World Shoulder Bag

Heavily quilted, this shoulder bag has a convenient inner pocket. Choose a color scheme for each "Around the World" block that radiates out from the center.

Instructions - p. 88

FRANCE

Fashion, pastries, embroidery…thinking of France evoked warm feelings expressed by delicate designs of curved appliqués and fun polka dots.

10 Macaroon Shoulder Bag

One side is solidly appliquéd with little circles reminiscent of macaroons. The solid shoulder strap completes the shape of the bag while the bright blue zipper pull adds a pop of color.

Instructions - p. 90

11 Orange Peel Handbag

I love this irregularly shaped bag. The front is a pieced orange peel pattern while the back uses the same background fabric, but is left in its simplistic beauty.

Instructions - p. 92

12 Polka Dot Tea Time Handbag

Appliquéd with teapots, cups and saucers, this bag is perfect to take along to a tea party. The flap with the circular cut-out mimics the polka dots of the background fabric, making it a unique conversation piece.

Instructions - p. 94

13 Appliquéd Granny Bag

The exquisitely detailed appliqué and embroidered border at the top of the bag makes this granny bag eye-catching and begs a closer look.

Instructions - p. 96

ITALY

Italy is a country of contrasts. Today, it is known as much for its new and modern designs as it is for the wonderfully historic buildings and architecture. Each time I visit I am inspired by the composition and color around me. I had a lot of fun designing these bags as the ideas flowed easily.

14 Modern Structural Bag

I designed this bag while thinking of Italian architectural structures. I made fabric tubes, then sewed them to the sides of the bag. Using either hand-dyed or fabric with color gradation gives the bag an extra level of interest.

Instructions - p. 98

15 Chic Hexagon Handbag

This egg-shaped bag is made up of four different units of pieced hexagons. The lining can be easily seen so be sure to use a fun fabric that makes you happy.

Instructions - p. 100

16 Woolen Waist Pouch

Pieced together with assorted scraps of wool, this waist pouch boasts an appliquéd cross, stitched on with sashiko-like stitches. It is perfect for a day out about town.

Instructions - p. 102

17 Contemporary Shoulder Bag

Modern and singular, this pitcher-shaped bag has easy access. The appliquéd bars are carefully matched up to give a contemporary feel to the design.

Instructions - p. 104

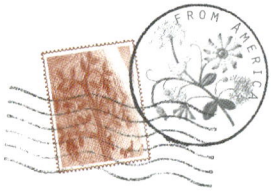

UNITED STATES OF AMERICA

I was first introduced to patchwork and quilting in America. I saw many different kinds of quilts and met so many people who love this artistic form of expression. Historically represented by traditional blocks and appliqué, there are almost too many patterns to count. I have some favorite designs that I seem to come back to time and time again...full of wonder and charm, they never get old.

18 Basket Block Pouchette

Pieced and appliquéd basket patterns are always charming to me and have become favorites of mine. This easy-to-sew pouchette features a simple basket block. The easy access bag design is perfect for strolling around your neighborhood or to take on a trip.

Step-by-Step Instructions - p. 56

19 Patchwork Flowers Shoulder Bag

An ideal complement for shopping or on a journey, this shoulder bag holds more than you think. By carefully color-planning and cutting the hexagons, unique flowers appear when sewn together. The gusset is fairly wide and unusually embellished with appliquéd bias strips.

Instructions - p. 106

20 Birdhouses in a Tree Handbag

A variety of birds gather together near their houses hanging from branches in the tree, tweeting happily despite the cat watching from below. The two handles are made of canvas topped with faux suede.

Instructions - p. 108

21 Orange Peel Grommet Handbag

The classic orange peel design appliquéd in a circular pattern in fun and funky-colored fabrics stand out on a black-striped background. The simple gusset and oversized grommets make a nice design counterpart.

Instructions - p. 110

Foundational Techniques
for beautiful handwork

It is important to learn the most basic foundations of any craft. These instructions will help give you the basic techniques and mastering them will allow you to create beautiful hand-made items.

Appliqué

Piecework

Embroidery

Quilting

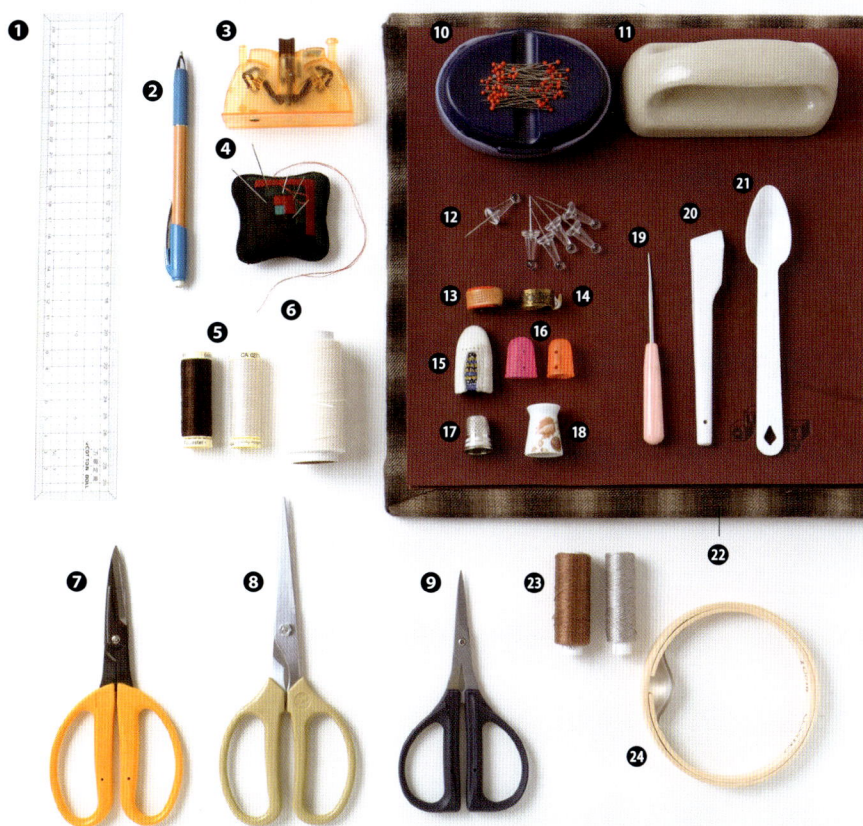

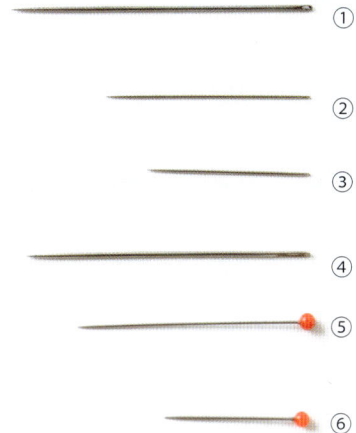

Pins & Needles

① Basting Needle - A long needle used for basting.

② Appliqué or Piecing Needle - Easy to appliqué with, as they tend to bend with use. Used to piece together fabric.

③ Quilting Betweens Needles - Shorter than sharps, used for quilting.

④ Embroidery Needle - Perfect for embroidery stitches.

⑤ Straight Pins - An easy-to-use longer straight pin with a small head.

⑥ Appliqué Pins - A short pin, with a small head that won't get in the way while you appliqué.

Essential Quilting Notions & Tools

❶ Ruler - Used to trace straight lines when transferring patterns. Rulers with markings made for quilters are useful.

❷ Marking Pencil - Used to transfer patterns to either paper or fabric or for marking quilting lines. Mechanical pencils allow for greater precision and lines disappear with water.

❸ Needle Threader - A simple tool making it easier to thread needles.

❹ Pincushion - Convenient for keeping pre-threaded needles with a variety of colors when doing appliqué.

❺ Thread - Used for piecing, stitching, quilting and machine sewing. Use shades of thread that closely match the fabric color.

❻ Basting Thread - Used for basting.

❼ Scissors (a pair specifically for paper) - They will last longer if each pair is used for specific things, such as for paper, fabric or thread.

❽ Scissors (a pair specifically for fabric).

❾ Scissors (a pair specifically for thread).

❿ Magnetic Pincushion - Conveniently keeps your pins and needles handy.

⓫ Weights (paperweights, beanbags, etc.) - Used to weigh down a small quilt when quilting.

⓬ Push Pins - Useful to keep layers from shifting when getting ready to baste the quilting sandwich. The longer the pin, the better.

⓭ Adjustable Thimble - To help push the needle and thread through thick sections when quilting.

⓮ Ring Cutter - Conveniently worn on your left (or right) thumb and used for cutting threads as you are working.

⓯ Leather Thimble - Slip this over a metal thimble on your middle finger as you work to keep work from slipping.

⓰ Rubber Thimbles - Wear on your right index finger during quilting or appliqué to help grab the needle and reduce slippage.

⓱ Metal Thimble - Used to push the needle through the cloth when quilting. (Flat and Round Head).

⓲ Porcelain Thimble - Useful and beautiful, once you get used to it.

⓳ Awl - To mark corner points when transferring and drawing patterns.

⓴ Seam Pressing Tools - Used to press seam allowances down, in lieu of ironing when working with appliqué pieces. (Finger Presser, Hera Markers).

㉑ Spoon - Often used when pin-basting a quilt. Diaper pins are easy to use for this method.

㉒ Non-Slip Board - The non-slip surface board is used when marking fabric or when using the fabric pressing tool to turn under the seam allowances. The soft side backed with batting and fabric can be used as a mini ironing surface.

㉓ Embroidery Floss - Used for embroidery stitches. If you can buy 2-strand on a spool, it can also be used in your sewing machine.

㉔ Embroidery Hoop - Used to secure fabric when doing embroidery.

*Other notions and tools I use: hoops (quilting), quilt stand (used when quilting large projects), heavyweight paper (for templates/patterns), tracing paper, light table, cellophane tape, iron, spray adhesive.

Appliqué

Appliquéing stems

1

Lay your fabric, wrong side up, on the non-slip board. Use the ruler to draw a reference line on a 45° angle on the fabric.

2

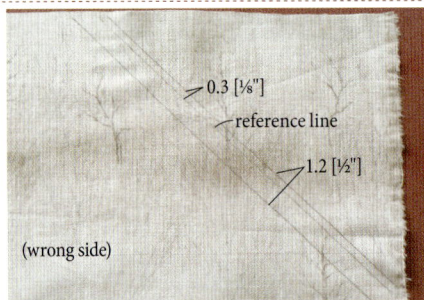

Draw two parallel lines next to the reference line. The first should be 0.3 cm [⅛"] to one side of the reference line. The second should be 1.2 cm [½"] on the opposite side.

3

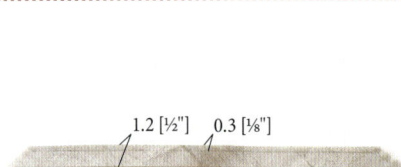

Using your ruler and a rotary cutter or scissors, cut out the fabric for the stem on the outermost lines. Cutting the fabric out on a 45° angle creates bias fabric, making it easy to manipulate around curves.

4

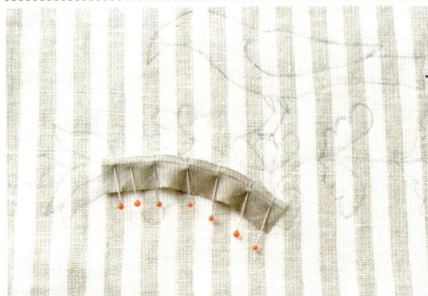

Take the bias strip and pin in place on the marked background fabric, matching the fold (reference) line to the drawn pattern.

5

Using a running stitch, begin and end stitches 0.5 cm [¼"] from the ends.

6

Backstitch at either end to secure the stitches in place.

7

Fold the bias strip over right side out and finger press the stem into place.

8

Use the finger presser tool and press down firmly along the handsewn seam.

9

Turn the raw edge of the bias strip under, the width of the stem, matching the fold to the line drawn on the background fabric.

10

Begin to appliqué the stem down starting 0.5 cm [¼"] from the end and using a blindstitch (see p. 73).

11

Use the tip of the needle to "needle-turn" the seam allowance under as you work. Stitch to within 0.5 cm [¼"] of the end and secure the stitches.

12

Using this method, it is easy to appliqué any width or length of fabric with precision.

Appliquéing Heart Shapes

13

Begin by appliquéing two narrow stems in place on the background fabric. Prepare the fabric piece for the heart design with the markings on the right side of the fabric.

14

Pin the heart in place, matching the markings on the appliqué piece to the design drawn on the background fabric.

15

Pick a gentle curve to begin your work and needle-turn the seam allowance under to the marked line. Insert the needle from the back of the appliqué.

16

Using a blindstitch, appliqué the heart down to the background fabric being sure to match the placement lines.

17

Stitch up to within 0.5 cm [¼"] of the top of the heart shape. Make one snip within the "v" of the seam allowance.

18

You can see the snipped seam allowance from the right side.

19

Turn the snipped seam allowance under with the tip of the needle.

20

Continue to blindstitch to where the snip was made. Since there is no seam allowance where the snip was made, bring the tip of the needle to the front and take at least two very tiny stitches to secure the inverted point.

21

As you begin to sew up around the inside curve, needle-turn the edges under, holding the piece in place with your thumb. Blindstitch up the curve.

22

Continue to blindstitch around the heart.

23

Stop stitching just before you reach the marking for the bottom point of the heart.

24

With the tip of your needle, turn the seam allowance under tight against the last stitch you took at the bottom point.

25

Once again, with the tip of your needle, turn the seam allowance under along the marked line. Turning the seam allowance under in this 2-step method should allow for the easiest and smoothest sharp corner.

26

Use the methods described above to appliqué any shapes that have curves, inverted "v" areas or sharp points.

Appliquéing Diamond Shapes

27

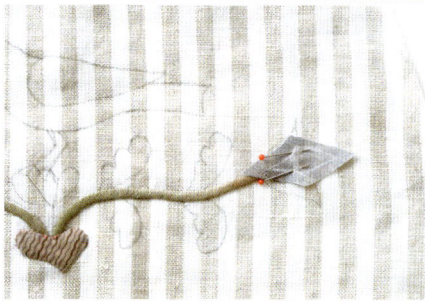

With the right side facing up, pin the diamond-shaped appliqué piece on the background fabric. Match the marked lines on the piece to the marked pattern lines on the background fabric.

28

Start the needle at one of the side points of the diamond and begin to blindstitch along the straight edge until you come to the first sharp end point.

29

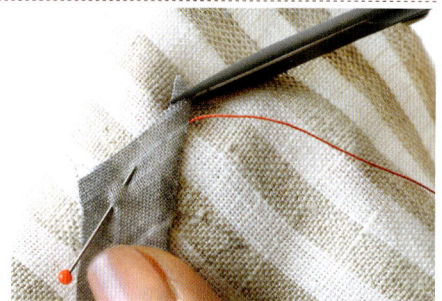

Carefully snip off the rabbit ear, as shown.

30

With the tip of your needle, turn the seam allowance under once.

31

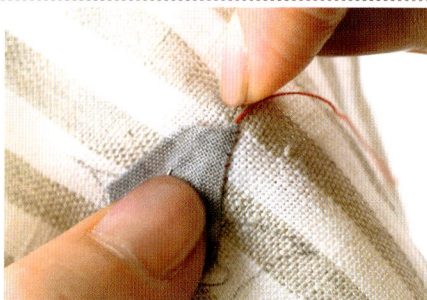

Using the tip of your needle, turn the seam allowance under again, evening out the seam allowance underneath while holding the appliqué in place with your thumb.

32

Once again, with the tip of your needle, manipulate the seam allowance tight against the last stitch you took at the sharp end point so that you have a very sharp and perfect point.

33

Begin blindstitching along the marked line to the next side point.

34

leave open

Leave both of the sides open (unstitched) where it will be overlapped by another appliqué piece in order to keep the layers as flat as possible.

Appliqué

Appliquéing a Basket Handle

1

Prepare the background piece for the basket handle. Using the non-slip board, trace the template shape on the wrong side of the fabric.

2

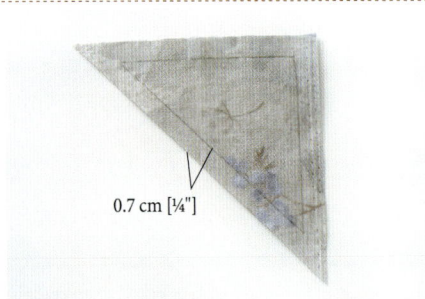

0.7 cm [¼"]

Cut the background piece out, adding 0.7 cm [¼"] for the seam allowance.

3

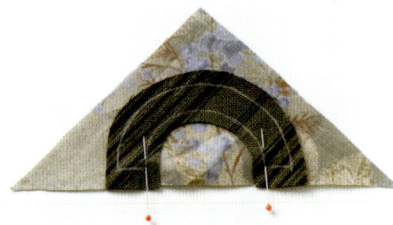

Prepare the basket handle piece. Using the non-slip board, trace the template shape on the right side of the fabric. Match the marked lines on the piece to the marked pattern lines on the background fabric.

4

While turning the seam allowance under with the tip of your needle, start to blindstitch the basket handle Begin to appliqué from the outer curve.

5

This shows the completed outside edge appliquéd to the background piece.

6

Using your scissors, clip into the inner curve of the handle, stopping 0.1 cm [¹/₁₆"] away from the marked sewing line.

7

With the tip of your needle, turn the seam allowance under at the marked line. Use your thumb to hold the seam allowance in place.

8

Blindstitch along the inner curve of the appliqué.

9

The completed basket handle.

Piecework

1

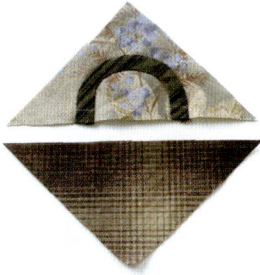

Prepare the fabric piece that will be sewn to the basket handle appliqué piece using the templates provided.

2

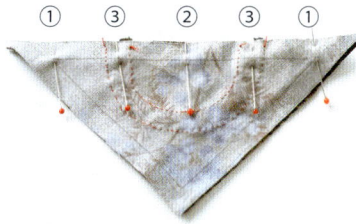

With right sides together, pin the pieces together matching the corner points. Add additional pins, matching the finished sewing lines as necessary, to hold the pieces together.

3

0.5 cm [¼"]

Begin stitching 0.5 cm [¼"] from the outside edge.

4

backstitch

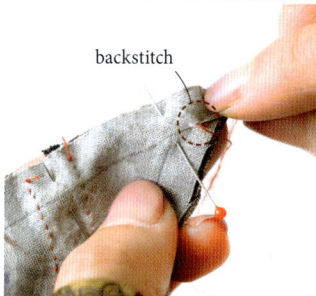

Take one backstitch to secure the end point.

5

Use a running stitch to sew along the marked finished sewing lines.

6

backstitch once

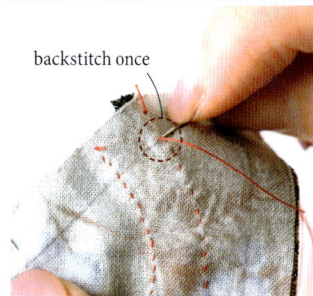

When you reach a section with additional fabric layers, it is best to take a single backstitch at the beginning and end of the area for increased strength.

7

0.5 cm [¼"]

Sew to within 0.5 cm [¼"] of the end and take a single backstitch to secure the stitching.

8

Trim the seam allowances down to 0.7 cm [¼"].

9

When hand-piecing seams, fold the finished seam to one side and press, leaving 0.1 cm [¹/₁₆"] showing over the fold. This helps to hide the seam when the piece is opened up.

10

The completed pieced section.

Embroidery

Appliqué the designs to the background fabric.

Thread the embroidery needle with the embroidery floss (or perle cotton, depending on the design) and knot the end.

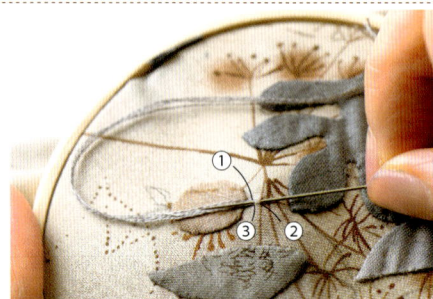

Outline Stitch

1

Begin the Outline Stitch by coming up from underneath the fabric at position ①, insert at position② and out again at position③.

2

Continue to stitch in the same manner, following the marked line on the background fabric.

3

The Outline Stitch is perfect for embroidering both straight and curving stems and lines.

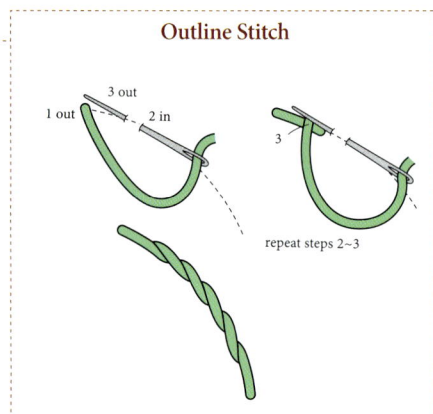

Outline Stitch

3 out
1 out   2 in

3

repeat steps 2~3

Double Laisy Daisy Stitch

1

Begin the Double Lazy Daisy Stitch by bringing your embroidery needle up at position①.

2

Insert the needle at position ② and bring it out at position ③. Bring the embroidery floss around under the tip of the needle back towards position ② and pull the needle all the way through.

3

In order to make the loop, insert the needle back into the fabric in the same spot where the stitch started and pull the floss gently, leaving the loop in place.

4

Repeat the loop stitch with a slightly smaller one inside the first one to create the "double" stitch.

5

This completes the Double Lazy Daisy Stitch.

Double Lazy Daisy Stitch

4 in

3 out

1 out 2 in

Laisy Daisy Stitch

3 out

2 in

4 in

1 out

Colonial Knot Stitch

1

Bring the tip of the needle out at the exact place where you want the stitch to show. Pull the floss all the way until the knot underneath is taut against the back.

2

Wrap the floss around the tip of the needle.

3

Then wrap the floss around the tip of the needle again to form a "figure eight" and pull taut down to the tip of the needle. Insert the needle back down just to the side of where you initially brought the needle out.

4

Bring the needle back up in the location where you want to see the next stitch, making sure to keep the floss taut until you pull it all the way through.

5

This completes one Colonial Knot Stitch. To get the look on the right, fill the space with as many Colonial Knot Stitches as can fit inside the marked circle.

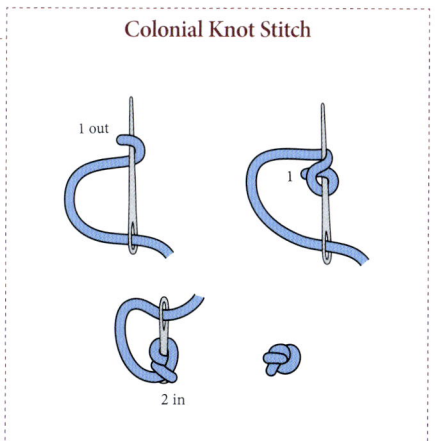

Colonial Knot Stitch

1 out

1

2 in

Quilting

Basting

1

Once you have completed the top, prepare the backing and the batting. With the wrong side up, smooth the backing fabric out on a flat surface and pin or tape it to hold it taut.

2

Begin by pinning or taping the four corners, followed by the center point of each side.

3

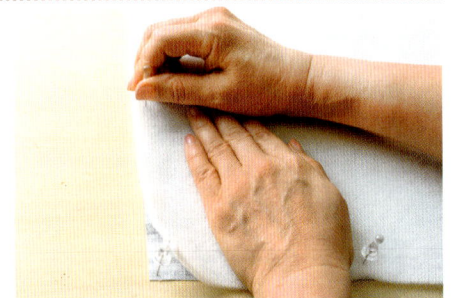

With the batting cut to the same size as the backing fabric, lay it on top of the backing and re-pin or tape both layers to the flat surface.

4

Center the quilt top on top of the layers and pin down.

5

Now you are ready to begin the basting process.

6

Starting in the center of the quilt top with a length of knotted thread, baste all the way to the left edge. Use a spoon to help lift the needle from the surface as you baste.

7

Knot the thread at the edge and cut it, leaving a 2~3 cm [¾"~1¼"] tail. Repeat basting from the center out in a sunburst pattern following the order in the illustration to the right.

8

Your basted quilt sandwich should look like this when you are done. I often use a contrasting thread color to see it easily.

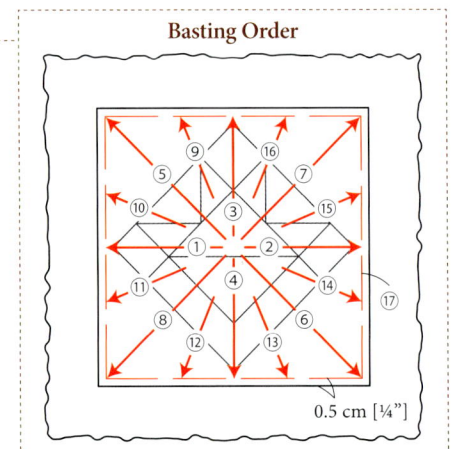

Basting Order

0.5 cm [¼"]

54

Quilting

9

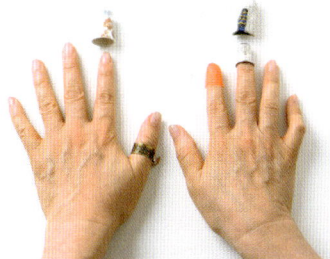

See the photo above for proper finger placement of quilting notions so as not to hurt your fingers while you quilt. There are many thimbles on the market, so find ones that are most comfortable for you when you work.

10

Using the non-slip board and weights, place the quilt as shown to keep it from moving while you quilt. Always start in the center of your quilt sandwich and work your way out toward the edges.

11

Knot the end of the thread and insert the needle into the quilt top and batting about 1 cm [⅜"] away from where you will begin the first stitch. Pull the thread through until the knot is lying on the surface of the quilt top. Gently tug the thread to pop the knot through the quilt top to bury it in the batting.

12

Before you begin quilting, take one little stitch without going all the way through to the backing.

13

Insert the needle again at the first stitch perpendicular to the top and pull through the back, coming up very close to the first stitch. Insert the needle down again until you feel the tip of the needle with your finger under the quilt and immediately come back up.

14

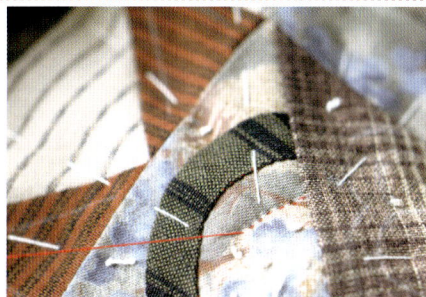

Repeat this rocking motion until you have several stitches on your needle. Then use the thimble to push the needle through the quilt. Pull the thread to even the tension. Repeat until the end of your quilting line.

15

When you reach the end of your quilting line, backstitch into the preceding space, bringing the needle up to create the final stitch.

16

Insert the needle in the last stitch again and work the needle through the batting, bringing the tip of the needle out about 1 cm [⅜"] away from the last stitch. Carefully cut the thread close to the quilt top.

Quilting Step-by-Step

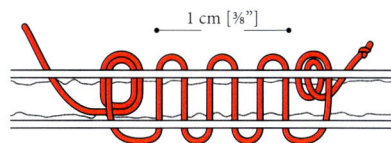

1 cm [⅜"]

Shown on p. 36

A Step-by-Step Lesson

The template/pattern can be found on Side D of the pattern sheet inserts.

Basket Block Pouchette

This is a cute, yet practical, little pouchette with a hidden zippered pocket accessible from the outside. I placed a favorite basket block on point within a pieced frame. The light-colored background of the basket helps the block design pop.

Materials

Assorted fat quarters or scraps consisting of checks, stripes and patterns (upper and lower bag front)

Dk brown homespun - 3.5 × 50 cm [1⅜" × 19¾"] (bias binding for bag opening)

Brown homespun - 3.5 × 25 cm [1⅜" × 9¾"] (bias binding for upper front bag zipper opening)

Green stripe - 25 × 27 cm [9¾" × 10⅝"] (bag back)

Grey print - 110 × 30 cm [43¼" × 11¾"] (lining, facing)

Batting - 60 × 40 cm [23⅝" × 15¾"]

1 Zipper - 18 cm [7⅛"] long

Leather cord - 0.5 × 12 cm [¼" × 4¾"] (loops for straps)

Waxed cord - 10 cm [4"] (zipper pull)

1 Wooden button - 2 cm [¾"] (zipper pull)

1 Leather strap - 1.5 cm [⅝"] wide

Dimensional Diagram

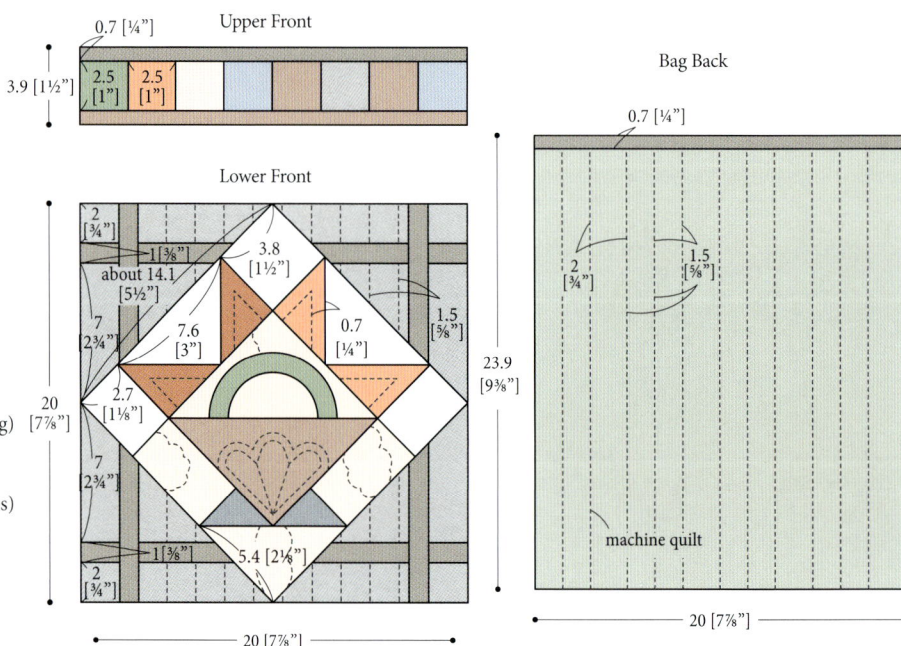

Upper Front

0.7 [¼"]

3.9 [1½"]

2.5 [1"]   2.5 [1"]

Lower Front

2 [¾"]

1 [⅜"]

3.8 [1½"]

about 14.1 [5½"]

7 2¾"

7.6 [3"]

0.7 [¼"]

1.5 [⅝"]

2.7 [1⅛"]

7 2¾"

20 [7⅞"]

1 [⅜"]

5.4 [2⅛"]

2 [¾"]

20 [7⅞"]

Bag Back

0.7 [¼"]

2 [¾"]

1.5 [⅝"]

23.9 [9⅜"]

machine quilt

20 [7⅞"]

Piecing the Pouchette Front

1

Using the pattern on the pattern sheet inserts, cut out each piece, being sure to add 0.7 cm [¼"] seam allowances. Lay them out (as shown above) to make sure you have all the necessary pieces.

2

Begin by starting with the basket in the center. Sew the basket base pieces and background rectangles next to them together (see instructions for piecing on p. 51). Press the seams toward the basket bases.

3

Appliqué the basket handle to the background, then sew that section to the basket piece (detailed instructions are on pp. 50-51). Press the seam toward the basket.

4

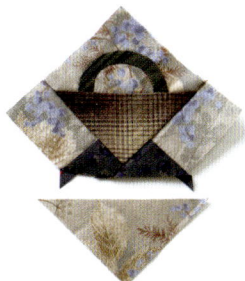

Sew the background triangle to the bottom of the pieced basket section and press the seam toward the basket base.

5

This completes the center part of the basket block.

6

Sew the upper diagonal sections of the block together. Lay them out before sewing to make sure you have the pieces in the correct position.

7

Sew the two smaller triangles to the larger inverted triangle for both sides. Press the seams toward the darker red fabric.

8

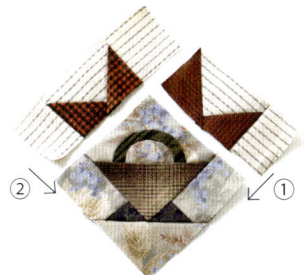

With right sides together, sew ① to the top right of the center basket section. Press the seams toward the darker red fabric. Then sew ② to the top left of the block.

A Step-by-Step Lesson

57

9

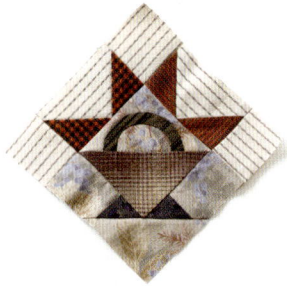

This completes the center section of the pattern. Press seams toward the basket.

10

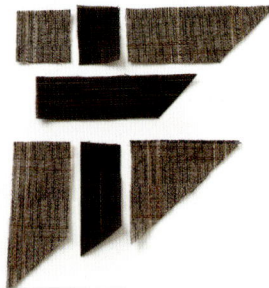

Lay out the pieces that make up each of the four corner frame sections.

11

Sew the top three pieces and bottom three pieces together as shown. Press the seams toward the skinny center piece for both sections.

12

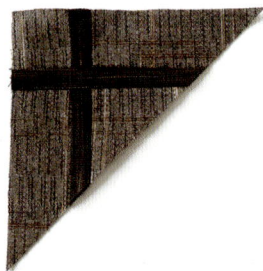

Sew the three sections together and press the seams toward the skinny center piece.

13

Make all four corner triangle sections.

14

Finish the lower front of the bag front by sewing the corner triangles to the center basket block. Press the seams toward the center.

2 Quilting the Pouchette Front

15

Cut out each of the squares to piece together the upper front. Sew them together, side by side, and press the seams in one direction.

16

Using a marking pencil that will show on the fabric, begin to draw the quilting lines.

17

Mark all the quilting lines on the lower front of the pieced front.

Tip

As quilted pieces tend to shrink somewhat, check both the length of the zipper and the overall dimensions before the next steps of sewing it together.

18

upper front
3 [1¼"]
3 [1¼"]
lower front
3 [1¼"]

Cut the batting and lining for both the lower front and the upper front sections 3 cm [1¼"] bigger on all sides. With wrong sides together and batting in between, baste; quilt both pieces. See p. 54 for step-by-step instructions.

19

back and lining
3 [1¼"]
3 [1¼"]

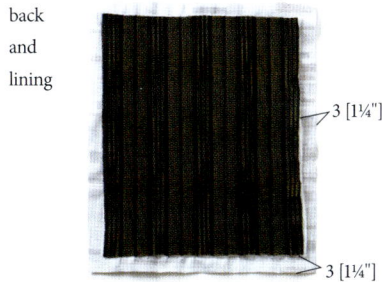

Cut the batting and lining for the back 3 cm [1¼"] bigger on all sides. With wrong sides together and batting in between, baste; machine quilt. Trim the excess batting on the back close to the fabric edges.

20

Measure the dimensions of the lower front again after the quilting (referencing the dimensional diagram). If necessary, redraw the finished sewing lines, using the four corners of the center block.

3 Sewing the Zipper to the Lower Front Section

21

zipper center
lower front center point

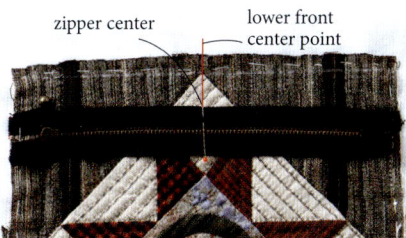

Measure the zipper to find the center point and mark it. With right sides together, align the center of the zipper to the center point of the lower front. Then keeping the center points together, align the edges and pin in place.

22

0.7 [¼"]

Sew the zipper tape to the lower front piece.

23

Trim the batting close to the edge of the zipper tape across the top.

24

Fold the zipper up, pressing the sewn zipper tape and seam allowance down toward the lower front piece.

25

lining (right side)
0.7 [¼"]

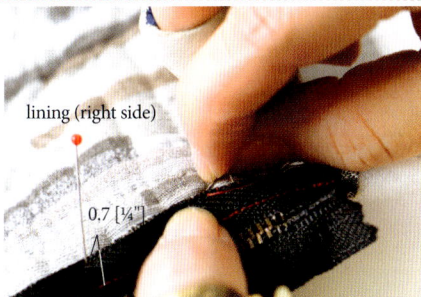

Cover the lining fabric with the edge of the zipper tape. Blindstitch the edge of the tape, catching only the lining fabric as you sew.

26

The lower front section (outer pocket) is complete.

A Step-by-Step Lesson

4 Making the Bias Binding

27

Lay the fabric on the non-slip board and fold down at an angle, using the markings on your ruler to achieve a perfect 45°.

28

Fold the fabric back up keeping the ruler at the 45° angle. Using a marking pencil, draw the first marking line that will be used as a reference line.

> **Tip**
>
> The points need to be offset by 0.7 cm [¼"] so that the edge will line up after it is sewn.

29

3.5 [1⅜"]   0.7 [¼"]

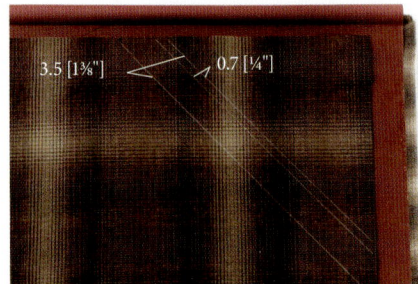

Draw an additional cutting line parallel to the reference line 3.5 cm [1⅜"] away. These will be your cutting lines. Use a different color marking pencil to draw the finished sewing line 0.7 cm [¼"] from the cutting line. (Repeat the marking of the cutting and sewing lines if making longer binding or needing additional bias strips.)

30

Cut the bias strip(s) on the cutting lines. Note that you will have the finished sewing line already marked from the previous step.

31

To make specific lengths of bias binding, you will need to sew the bias strips together. Take two bias strips and lay them crossed with right sides together, to create right angles. Match the edges and pin (the marked finished sewing lines should match up). Sew with a 0.7 cm [¼"] seam allowance.

32

Press the seam allowance open.

33

With right sides together, lay the bias strip on top of the upper front section with the batting against the wrong side of the upper front; pin in place.

34

0.7 [¼"]

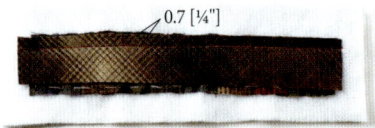

Sew from end to end with a 0.7 cm [¼"] seam allowance.

35

Trim the excess batting and seam allowances down to 0.7 cm [¼"].

36

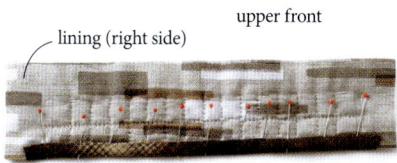

Fold the bias binding over twice and toward the lining, covering the raw edges. Pin in place.

37

Blindstitch the binding down to the lining fabric.

38

The upper front section (outer pocket) is now complete.

5 Sewing the Zipper to the Upper Front Section

39

Measure the dimensions of the upper front to make sure that the edges line up with the lower front piece.

40

With the right sides facing you, pin the upper front to the lower front, covering the zipper with the upper front binding.

41

Using a backstitch and catching only the batting and lining, sew the zipper to the upper front close to the zipper teeth. Then blindstitch the zipper tape to the lining fabric.

6 Making the Strap Loops

42

The inside lining (outer pocket) is complete.

43

Cut two pieces of leather cord to 12 cm [7⅛"]. Fold them in half and sew the ends by machine to secure.

44

The strap loops will be positioned on either side of the pouchette.

Sewing the Pouchette Together

45

In order to make certain the binding that covers the zipper stays in place, sew across the ends of the upper front bias binding through all thicknesses by machine or use a backstitch to secure.

46

23 [9"]

lining (right side)

27 [10⅝"]

pocket facing (right side)

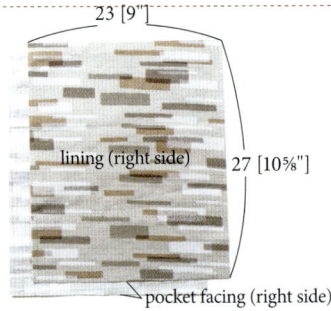

Cut two pieces of the facing fabric 23 × 27 cm [9" × 10⅝"]. This will make the lining of the outer pocket and inside of the pouchette.

47

pouchette front

back lining

pouchette back

With right sides together and aligning edges, lay the pouchette front and pouchette back together. Lay the facing/lining piece created in the previous step against the wrong side of the pouchette front. Note that if you are using the same fabric for the facing and lining, it won't matter which side faces up.

48

pocket facing

pouchette back

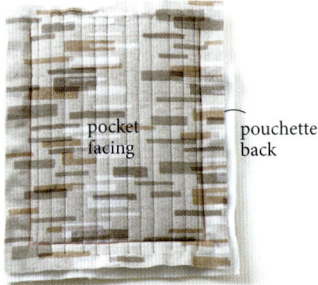

Sew along the finished sewing lines around the sides and bottom.

49

pouchette back lining

0.7 [¼"]

pocket facing/lining

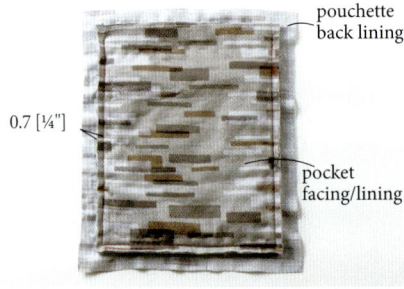

Trim the seam allowances from the three sewn sides down to 0.7 [¼"] except for the lining of the pouchette back. This will be used to bind the raw edges.

50

Turn the back lining over to the facing/lining side and fold twice to create the binding (covering the raw seams); pin in place.

51

Blindstitch the binding down to the lining.

52

trim here

When you get close to the corners, trim the folded binding as shown in the picture above. This will help you get neat corners with less thicknesses.

53

At each corner, fold the binding to create a perfect miter. Stitch each mitered corner down.

54

Continue to blindstitch the binding down to the lining.

55

Complete the opposite corner with the same mitering technique and finish binding the remaining side.

56

Turn the pouchette right side out. Gently work the bottom corners to get the desired shape.

8 Binding the Pouchette Opening

57

The pouchette body is complete.

58

Make the bias binding for the bag opening (see p. 60 for detailed instructions). With right sides together and aligning to the finished sewing lines, start on the back a little to the right of the side seam and pin the binding to the body, overlapping the ends by approximately 1 cm [⅜"].

59

Sew along the finished sewing line with a backstitch (or by machine). Leave 0.7 [¼"] beyond where the binding overlaps, then trim off the rest. Turn the trimmed end under 0.7 [¼"].

60

Fold the binding in half to meet the edge. Then fold again over the lining so that the folded binding edge covers the stitching line. Blindstitch down to the lining all around.

61

For a unique zipper pull, I removed the original zipper pull tab and replaced it with a button strung with waxed cord.

62

Snap a store-bought leather strap onto the strap loops to complete the pouchette.

Shown on p. 8

A Step-by-Step Lesson

The template/pattern can be found on Side A of the pattern sheet inserts.

This little pouch, made with a gusset and zipper tabs, has a cute motif of a little bird. If you are new to appliqué or want to brush up your skills, I have given detailed instructions, using this design as an example, from pp. 46 - 49.

Appliquéd Bird Pouch

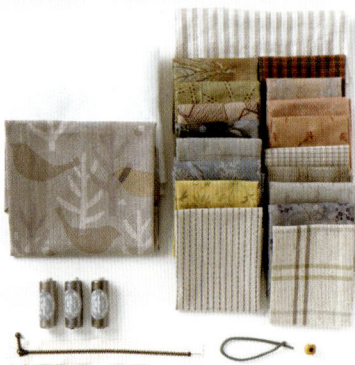

Materials

Assorted fat quarters or scraps consisting of checks, stripes and patterns (appliqué)
Homespun - 40 × 35 cm [15¾" × 13¾"]
   (pouch sides, appliqué background)
Beige stripe homespun - 3.5 × 25 cm [1⅜" × 9¾"]
   (make 2 pieces - bias binding for zipper opening)
Brown homespun - 28 × 8 cm [11" × 3⅛"] (bottom)
Check homespun- 10 × 15 cm [4" × 5⅞"] (zipper tabs)
Grey print - 35 × 35 cm [13¾" × 13¾"] (lining)
Batting - 35 × 35 cm [13¾" × 13¾"]
Fusible interfacing - 10 × 10 cm [4" × 4"]
1 Zipper - 16 cm [6¼"] long
Waxed cord - 10 cm [4"] (zipper pull)
1 Wooden button - 1 cm [⅜"] (zipper pull)
Embroidery floss - colors to match

Dimensional Diagram

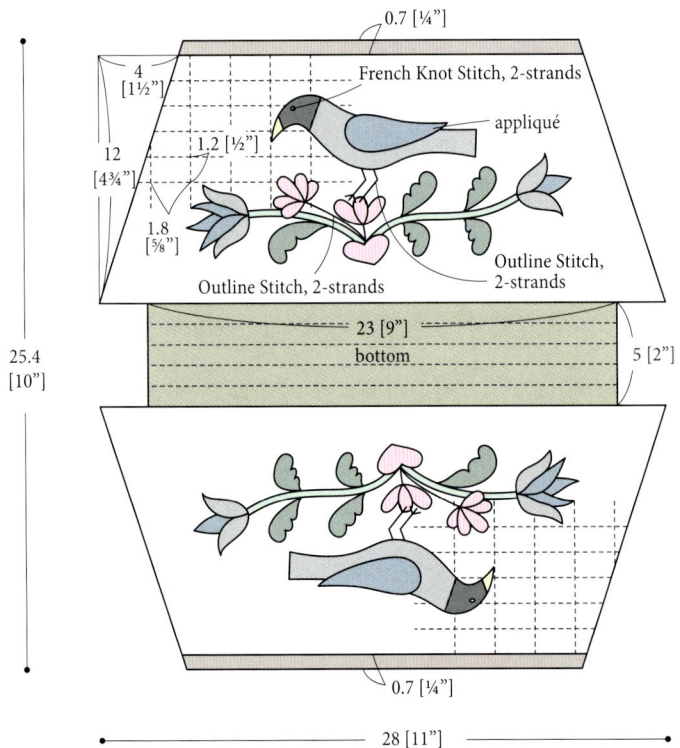

French Knot Stitch, 2-strands

appliqué

0.7 [¼"]

4 [1½"]

12 [4¾"]

1.2 [½"]

1.8 [⅝"]

Outline Stitch, 2-strands

Outline Stitch, 2-strands

23 [9"]
bottom

5 [2"]

25.4 [10"]

0.7 [¼"]

28 [11"]

Doing the Appliqué

1

Cut out the background fabric for the pouch sides, adding 0.7 cm [¼"] seam allowances. Find the appliqué pattern and transfer it to paper by a copy machine or by hand. Using a light table and a marking pencil, trace the design to the fabric. Repeat for the other side.

2

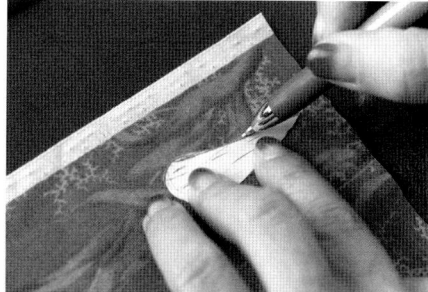

Make and cut out each of the pattern pieces for the design. Using a marking pencil, trace the outline of each piece to the fabric of your choice.

3

0.3 [⅛"]

(right side)

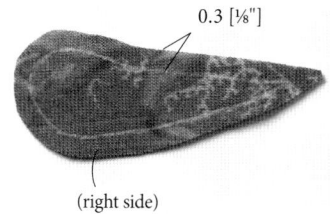

Cut out each appliqué pattern piece, adding 0.3 cm [⅛"] seam allowance all the way around.

4

Lay each pattern piece out (as shown above) to make sure you have all the necessary pieces.

5

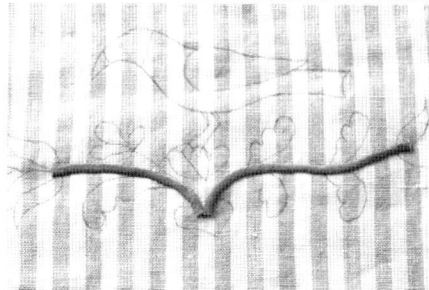

Begin by appliquéing the stems to the background fabric (see p. 46 for detailed instructions).

6

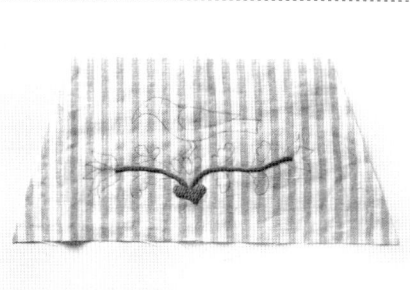

Next, appliqué the heart to the background. (see p. 47 for detailed instructions).

7

Continue by appliquéing the flowers to the ends of the stems.

8

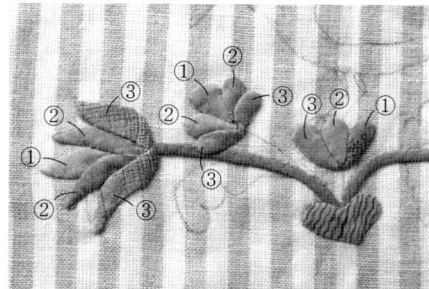

To layer the flower pieces correctly, follow the order laid out by the numbers in the picture above.

9

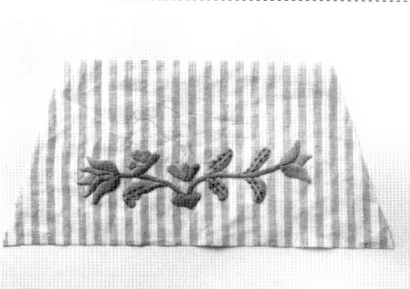

This completes the lower portion of the appliqué design.

10

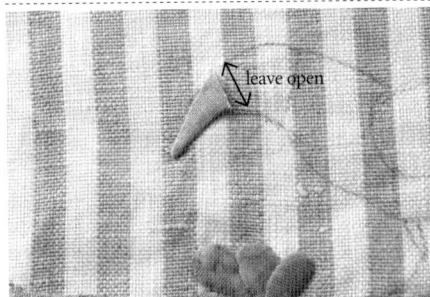

Begin to appliqué the bird by starting with the beak. Do not stitch down the section that will be overlapped by another piece. Leave it open to keep the fabric layers from getting too thick.

11

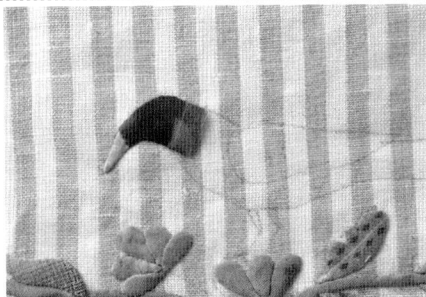

Appliqué the head on next, overlapping the beak and using the finished sewing line as a guide.

12

Continue by appliquéing the body in place.

13

Finish the appliqué portion of the bird by stitching on the wing.

14

At this point, begin to do the embroidery. Stitch the bird's feet (see pp. 52 - 53 for instructions on embroidery stitches).

15

Embroider a French Knot Stitch to make the bird's eye (see p. 78 for stitch instructions).

16

The appliqué and embroidery for the design are complete.

17

Repeat the instructions to make the back side of the pouch.

18

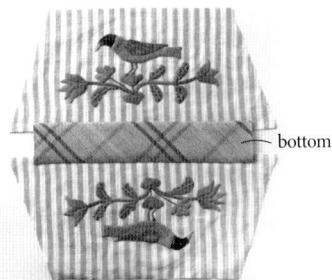

With right sides together, sew the pouch bottom to each of the pouch sides.

2 Quilting the Pouch

19

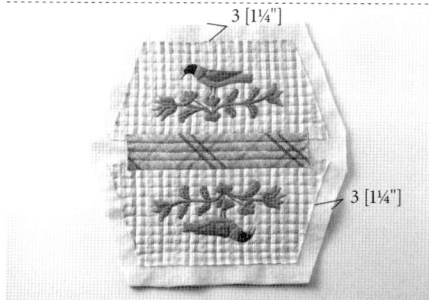

3 [1¼"]

3 [1¼"]

Cut the lining and batting 3 cm [1¼"] larger than the pouch body on all sides, baste. Quilt as desired (see p. 54 for detailed instructions on quilting).

20

The pouch body shown from the lining side.

21

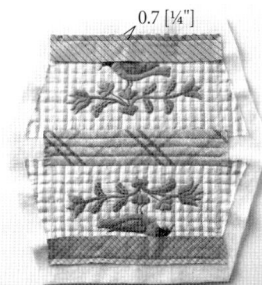

0.7 [¼"]

With right sides together and aligning edges, pin the bias strips to the zipper opening edges on both sides, then sew them down (see p. 60 for instructions on cutting bias strips and binding).

3 Sewing in the Zipper

22

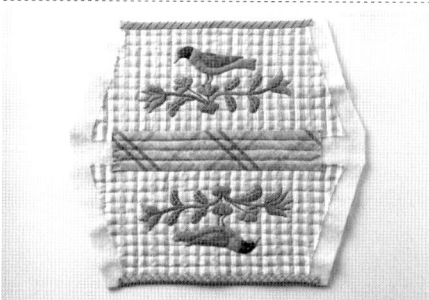

Trim the zipper opening seam allowances down to 0.7 [¼"]. Bind the edges with the bias binding and blindstitch down to the lining.

23

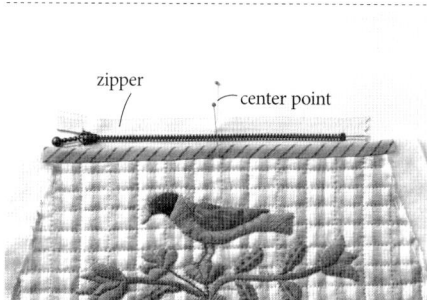

zipper

center point

Mark the center point of both the zipper opening (on both sides) as well as the zipper. With the right side of the zipper tape against the lining, align the center points.

24

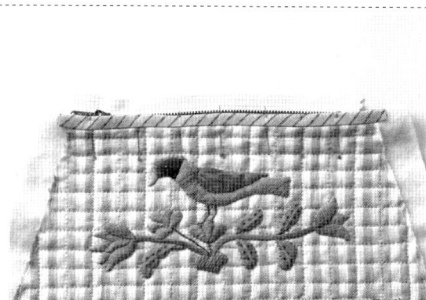

Pin the zipper in place.

4 Making the Gussets

25

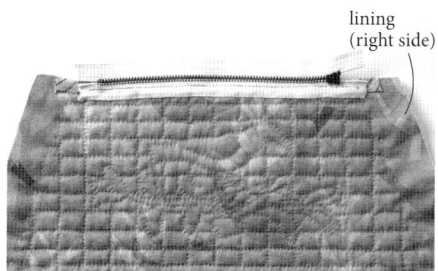

lining (right side)

Sew in the zipper using a backstitch close to the zipper teeth. Blindstitch the edge of the zipper tape to the lining.

26

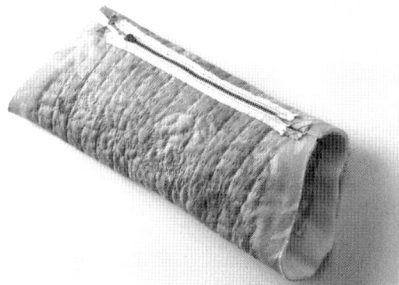

Repeat to sew the zipper to the other side of the pouch.

27

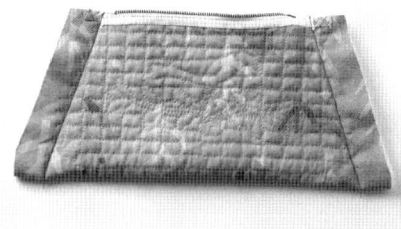

With right sides together and aligning edges, sew the side seams from top to bottom.

28

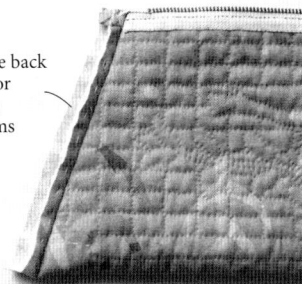

leave the back lining for binding the seams

Trim the seam allowances down to 0.7 [¼"] except for the lining of the pouch back. This will be used to bind the raw edges.

29

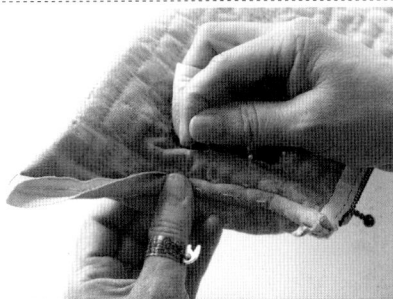

Turn the back lining over to the front and fold twice to create the binding (covering the raw seams); pin in place.

30

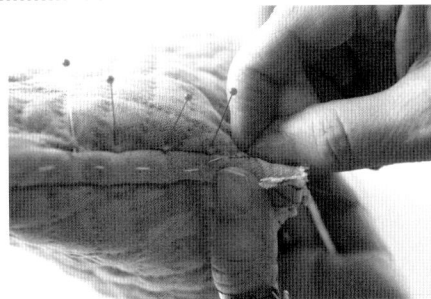

Blindstitch the binding down to the lining.

Tip

Be sure to center the side seams before sewing so that the pouch sides and gusset are even.

31

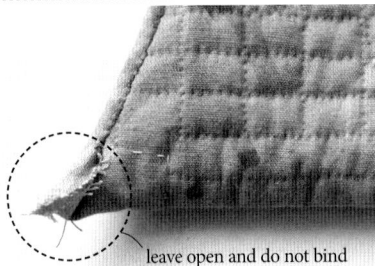

leave open and do not bind

Do not bind the last couple of centimeters (inches) at the bottom of the pouch. Once you sew across the ends to create the gussets, this will be cut off.

32

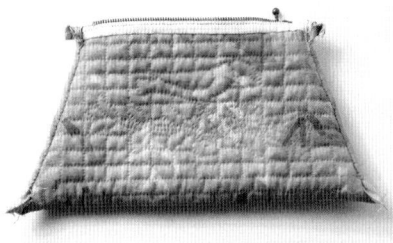

Repeat the previous steps to bind the other side seam of the pouch.

33

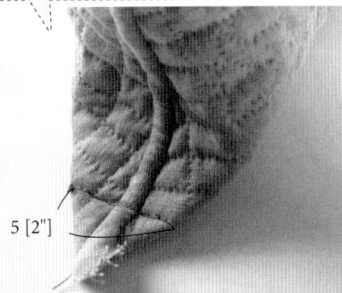

5 [2"]

Center the seam on the side of the bag and fold the corner tip into a triangle. With the triangle flattened down, use a marking pencil to draw a line 5 cm [2"] across. Sew across the line to create a gusset.

34

Repeat the previous step to make the gusset for the other side of the pouch.

35

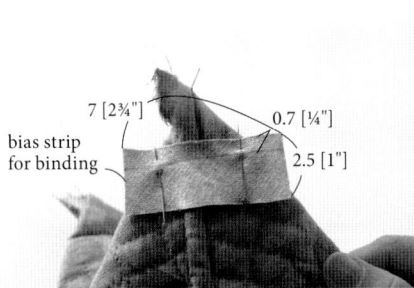

7 [2¾"]   0.7 [¼"]

bias strip for binding   2.5 [1"]

Cut a 2.5 × 7 cm [1" × 2¾"] bias strip to make the binding. With right sides together, sew the gusset and bias strip together along the finished sewing line with a 0.7 cm [¼"] seam allowance.

36

Cut the tip of the triangle off leaving a 0.7 cm [¼"] seam allowance.

37

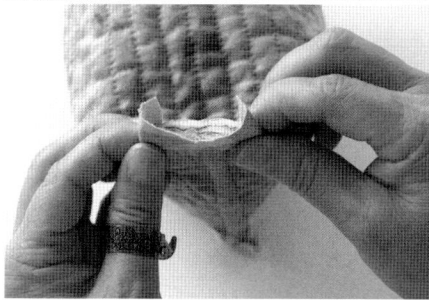

Fold the ends toward the inside and then fold the binding over the raw edge twice.

38

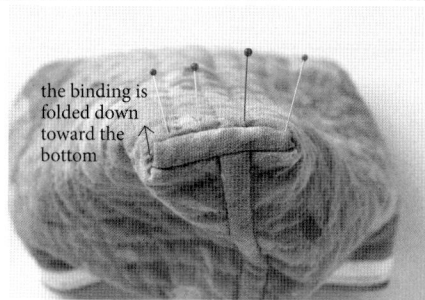

the binding is folded down toward the bottom

Pin the binding in place, then blindstitch it down to the lining.

39

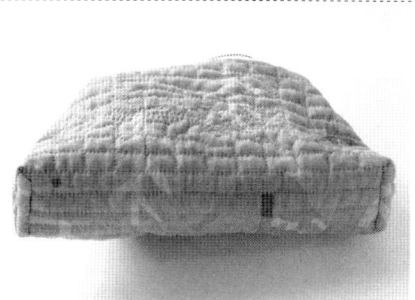

Repeat the previous step to bind the other side of the gusset to the bottom of the pouch.

5 Making the Zipper Tabs

40

3 [1¼"]

Center the zipper at the top of the bag; fold the corner tip into a triangle. With the triangle flattened down, use a marking pencil to draw a line 3 cm [1¼"] across. Sew across the line to create the top of the gusset.

41

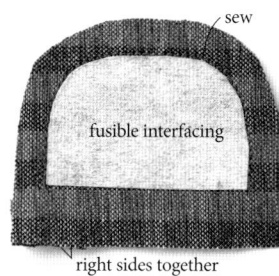

sew

fusible interfacing

right sides together

Cut four pieces of fusible interfacing (no seam allowance) and fuse to the wrong side of each of the four tab pieces. With right sides together, sew around the curve, leaving the bottom open.

42

Sew a running stitch in the seam allowance area; gently pull the thread to gather the outer edge of the tabs and tie off.

43

Turn both zipper tabs right side out. Turn the seam allowances on the bottom to the insides and press with an iron.

44

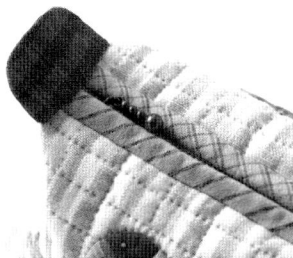

Center the zipper tab over the top gusset (from step 40 above) and blindstitch down all the way around. Repeat and blindstitch the remaining zipper tab to the other side of the pouch.

45

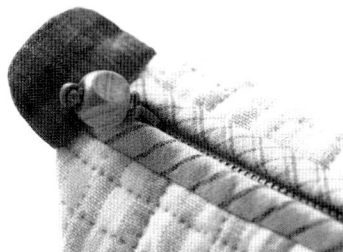

To create a unique zipper pull, remove the original zipper pull with pliers. Thread the waxed cord through the zipper clasp and add a bead; knot off the end to create the zipper pull.

46

The pouch is complete.

INDEX

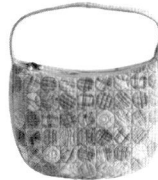

PROJECTS

All measurements listed for the following projects are in centimeters (cm) and inches [in brackets].

Seam allowances should be 0.7 cm [¼"] for all piecing unless otherwise specified. Seam allowances for appliqué pieces should be 0.3 cm [⅛"].

The dimensions of the finished projects are shown in the dimensional diagrams.

Note that the quilted pieces tend to shrink somewhat depending on the type of fabric used, the thickness of the batting, the amount of quilting and individual quilting technique. Please check the dimensions as you work and adjust seams as necessary.

There are projects where I specify areas that can be sewn or quilted by machine, however, all of the projects can be entirely sewn by hand.

Quilting Basics & Terminology

Sewing Marks - marks that are placed on fabric with fabric marking pencils to help line up pieces when sewing.

Appliqué - cutting and applying pieces of fabric to another background fabric to create designs.

Quilting Facing - fabric (often muslin) used against the back of batting when quilting the top to create the back layer of the quilt sandwich. Most often used when not wanting the quilting from the front to show through on the lining or backing.

Backing/Lining - fabric that is used for the back side of a quilt, bag or other project.

Blindstitch - used for appliqué and binding, tiny stitches are made by invisibly securing the appliqué to the background fabric.

Stitch-in-the-Ditch Quilting - quilting in the seam lines of a quilt or a hair's width outside of an appliqué.

Quilt Top - pieces that make up the front of a quilt or quilted project. Often made up of pieced or appliquéd quilt blocks.

Backstitch - the backstitch makes a very strong seam when sewing by hand.

Quilting - enclosing a warm layer of batting between two layers of fabric and kept in place by lines of stitching.

Batting - a layer of insulation that lies between the top and backing/lining of a quilt or quilted project. Often made of cotton, wool, bamboo or other fabrics, batting can be fairly thin or very lofty.

Running Stitch - the simplest of stitches to join two pieces of cloth.

Bag Opening/Zipper Opening Fabrics - the fabric used at the top opening edge of a bag or the zipper opening of a project. The fabric used is often a contrasting fabric.

Basting - sewing loose, large running stitches to hold two or more pieces of fabric together temporarily.

Fabric Strips - cotton quilting fabric cut into specific widths that can be sewn together for strip piecing.

Cut-to-Size - cutting pieces of fabric for a pattern with no added seam allowance.

Pleat - fabric that is folded back on itself; pressed and sewn in place along the seam line or edge.

Ladder Stitch - a hidden or mostly invisible stitch useful on straight edges or gentle curves.

Zipper Tabs - tabs sewn onto a pouch or bag at either end of a zipper. Easy to grab hold, they aid in opening and closing the zipper.

Knotting Thread - small knots that are made at the beginning and end of sewing to secure the thread and seams in place.

Background Fabric - fabric used as the background base to which appliqué is applied or embroidery is stitched.

Right Sides Together - sewing two pieces of fabric with the printed or outer ("right") side of the fabric laid against each other.

Binding - a cover for raw edges using a folded and stitched-down width of fabric on both the front and back. Most often made of bias fabric.

Piece - shaped pieces of fabric that will be stitched together; often triangular, square and diamond shapes.

Piecing - sewing fabric pieces (triangles, squares, etc.) together to create segments or blocks for a quilt top.

Gusset - adding a piece of fabric, or sewing seams into fabric to add breadth and provide expansion. Often used when making quilted bags and pouches.

Facing - fabric used for reinforcement, such as around bag openings.

Machine Quilting - quilting using a sewing machine rather than by hand.

One Patch Quilts - quilts that are constructed using a single, repeatable shape.

Basic Hand-Sewing Stitches and Methods

How to Tie a Knot

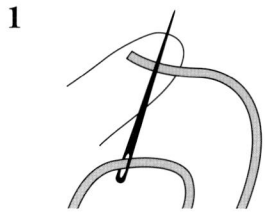

1

Lay the thread and needle across the tip of your index finger.

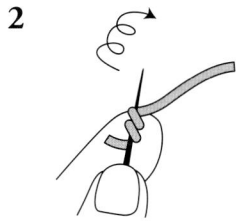

2

Holding the needle, wrap the thread around the tip twice.

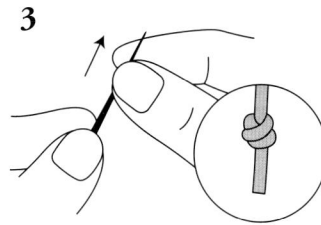

3

Pinching the wrapped thread between the thumb and index finger of your other hand, gently slide the needle up and out and pull the wrapped threads taut into a knot.

How to Secure the end of your Stitching

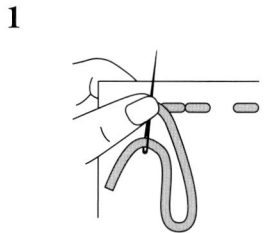

1

Press your thumb and needle against the final stitch where you need to secure the stitching.

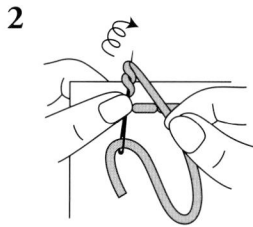

2

Wrap the thread around the tip of the needle twice, while holding it taut.

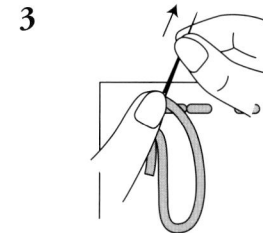

3

Pinch the wrapped threads under your thumb and slide the needle up and out until thread length is all the way through and creates a knot.

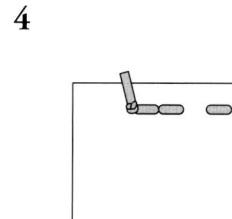

4

Cut, leaving a 2-3 cm [¾"-1¼"] tail.

Running Stitch

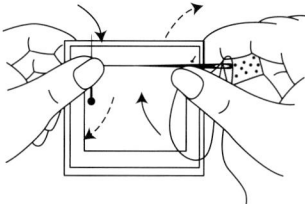

Holding the needle and thread in your right hand, work the needle in and out in tiny stitches while manipulating the fabric with your left. Pull the needle through, repeat to the end.

Backstitch

At the beginning

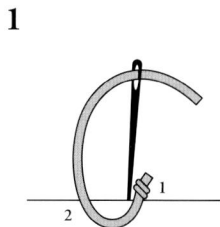

At the end

1

Bring the needle out on the right side at 1; back into the fabric at 2 and back out again to the right side at 1.

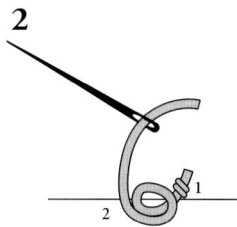

2

Go back into the fabric at 2.

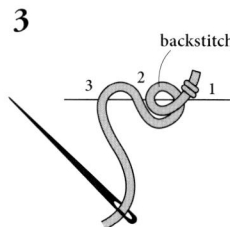

3

backstitch

Come back out to the right side at 3 and continue to backstitch to sew the rest of your seam.

backstitch

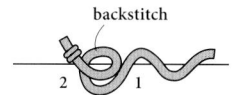

After your final stitch at 1, take two stitches in the same place and knot on the wrong side of the fabric at 2.

Ladder Stitch

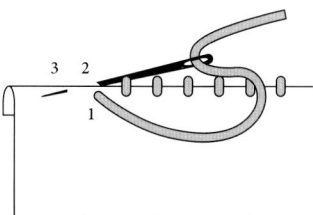

Bring the needle out at the fold of the appliqué edge at 1; insert the needle where the edge meets the background fabric at 2 and bring it back out again on the fold at 3.

Blindstitch

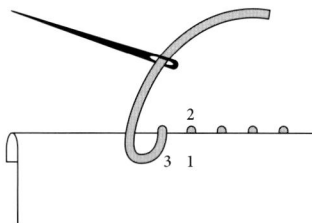

Bring the needle out at 1 under the edge of the turned-under seam allowance of the appliqué piece; catch the background fabric at 2 and come back up catching the seam allowance of the appliqué piece again. You will not be able to see any thread showing with this method.

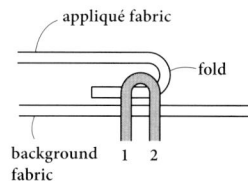

appliqué fabric

fold

background fabric

shown on p. 4

Songbird Handbag

> The template/pattern can be found on Side A of the pattern sheet inserts.

Materials

Assorted fat quarters or scraps consisting of checks, stripes and patterns (for appliqué, zipper pull and facing)
Beige print (bag front appliqué background) 35×35 cm [13¾" × 13¾"]
Beige print (bag back) 35×35 cm [13¾" × 13¾"]
Beige homespun (gusset) 95×15 cm [37⅜" × 5¾"]
Homespun (lining) - 95×70 cm [37⅜" × 27½"]
Batting - 95×50 cm [37⅜" × 19¾"]
Brown check homespun (bias binding) 3.5×30 cm [1⅜" × 11¾"]
Fusible interfacing - 90×40 cm [35⅜" × 15¾"]
Double-sided fusible interfacing -20×30 cm [7⅞" × 11¾"]
1 Zipper - 30 cm [11¾"] long
Handles (leather or faux-leather) - 1 pair
1 Wooden button (zipper pull)
Embroidery floss - colors to match

Directions

1 Cut out the pattern pieces including the lining, facing, batting and fusible interfacing if called for.
2 Appliqué and embroider the design to the bag front background piece.
3 With wrong sides together, layer the appliquéd bag front and the bag front lining with batting in between; baste and quilt. Fuse the interfacing to the wrong side of the bag back lining. With wrong sides together, layer the bag back and the bag back lining with batting in between; baste and quilt.
4 Baste the handles to the top edges of the bag front and bag back; with lining sides together, baste the inside pocket to the bag back.
5 Fuse the interfacing to the wrong side of the gusset lining. With wrong sides together, layer the gusset and the gusset lining with batting in between; baste and quilt.
6 Create the zipper facing and sew the zipper to the wrong side of the facing.
7 Sew the bottom center of the gusset together.
8 Align the bag front and bag back with the gusset using the marks as guides; baste; sew. Trim the seam allowances except for the gusset lining; use the lining to bind the raw edges; blindstitch down to the lining to finish.

Dimensional Diagram

Bag Front

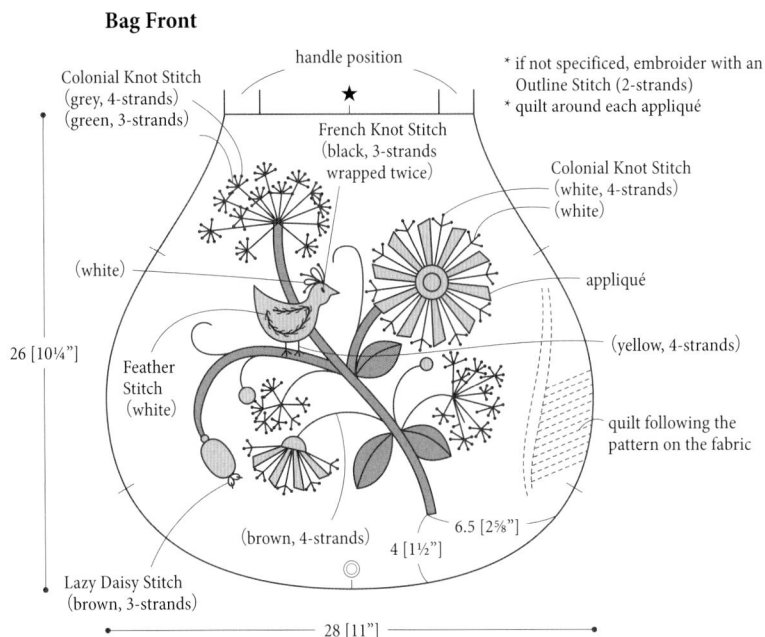

Bag Back

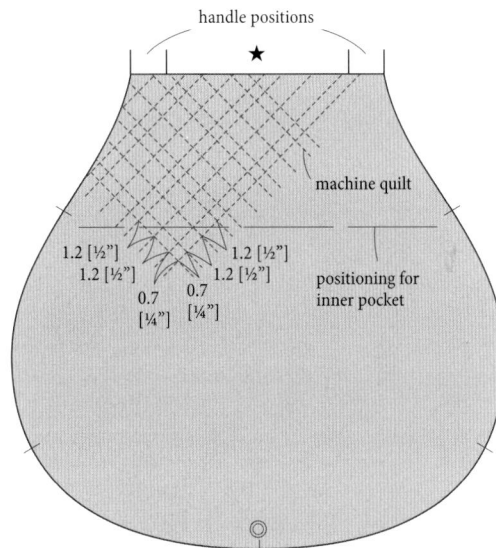

Gusset

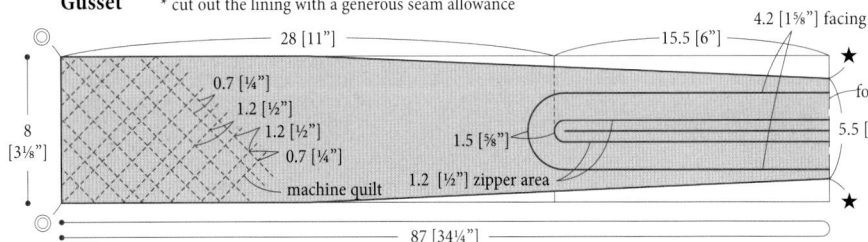

Facing

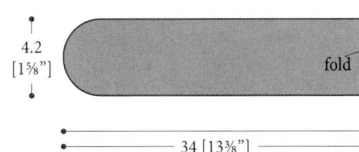

Bag Front

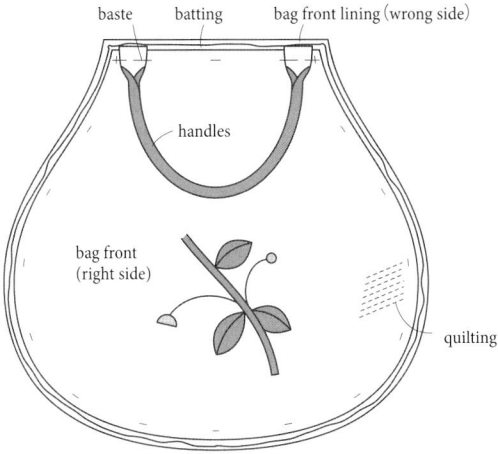

baste   batting   bag front lining (wrong side)

handles

bag front (right side)

quilting

Bag Back

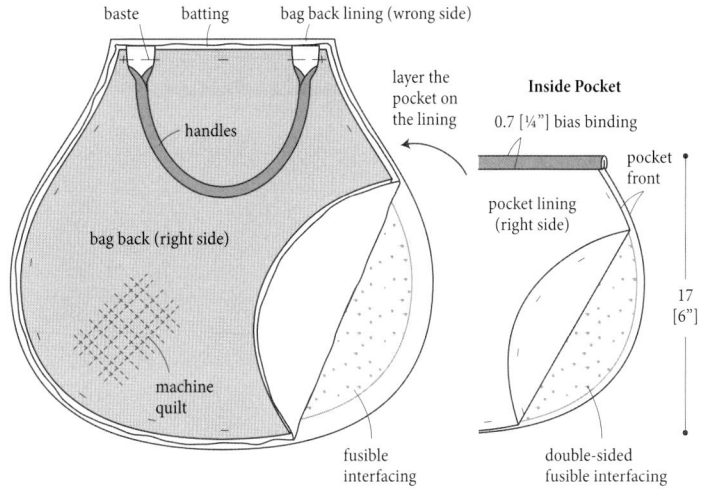

baste   batting   bag back lining (wrong side)

handles

layer the pocket on the lining

bag back (right side)

machine quilt

fusible interfacing

Inside Pocket

0.7 [¼"] bias binding

pocket front

pocket lining (right side)

17 [6"]

double-sided fusible interfacing

Gusset

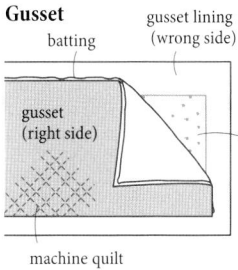

gusset lining (wrong side)

batting

gusset (right side)

fusible interfacing

machine quilt

Sewing the Facing

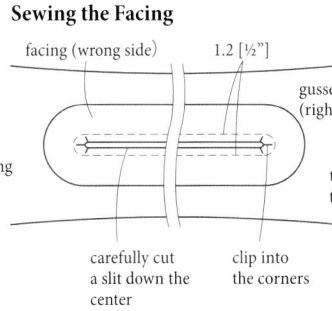

facing (wrong side)   1.2 [½"]

gusset lining (right side)

carefully cut a slit down the center

clip into the corners

turn the facing to the right side

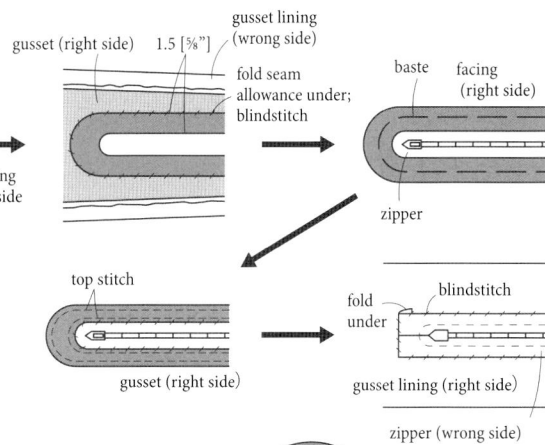

gusset (right side)   1.5 [⅝"]

gusset lining (wrong side)

fold seam allowance under; blindstitch

baste   facing (right side)

zipper

top stitch

gusset (right side)

fold under

blindstitch

gusset lining (right side)

zipper (wrong side)

Sewing the Bag Together

sew the bottom of the gusset together, then matching marks, pin the bag front and bag back to the gusset; baste; sew

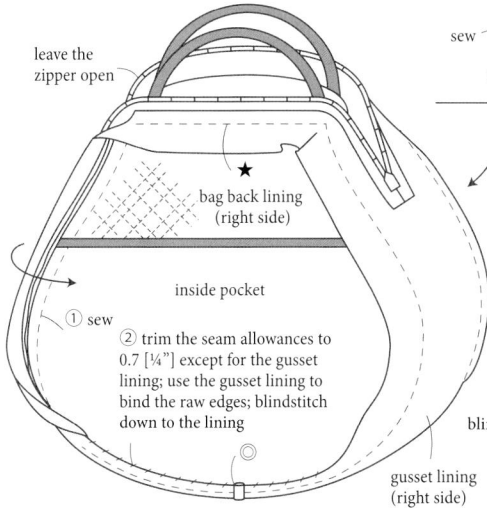

leave the zipper open

bag back lining (right side)

★

inside pocket

① sew

② trim the seam allowances to 0.7 [¼"] except for the gusset lining; use the gusset lining to bind the raw edges; blindstitch down to the lining

gusset lining (right side)

Sewing the Bottom of the Gusset

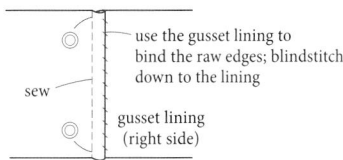

sew

use the gusset lining to bind the raw edges; blindstitch down to the lining

gusset lining (right side)

Zipper Pull

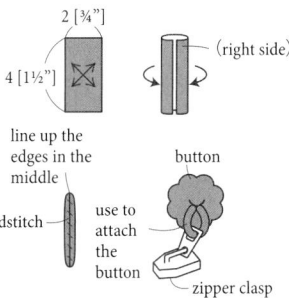

2 [¾"]

4 [1½"]

(right side)

line up the edges in the middle

blindstitch

button

use to attach the button

zipper clasp

Completed Bag

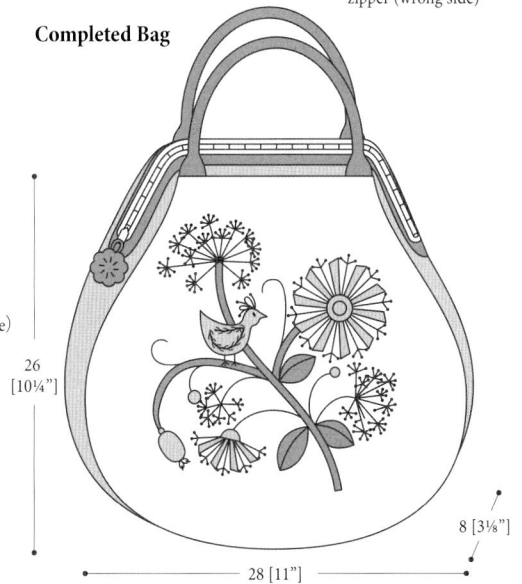

26 [10¼"]

8 [3⅛"]

28 [11"]

shown on p. 6

2 Floral Appliqué Boston Bag

The template/pattern can be found on Side A of the pattern sheet inserts.

Materials

Assorted fat quarters or scraps (appliqué including zipper tabs)
Beige stripe (pocket front, bag back, gusset, zipper pull) - 110 × 60 cm [43¼" × 23⅝"]
Beige plaid (bag front, bag lining) - 110 × 40 cm [43¼" × 15¾"]
Batting - 90 × 65 cm [35⅜" × 25⅝"]
Light green (bias binding) - 3.5 × 40 cm [1⅜" × 15¾"]
Beige print (inside bag bias binding) - 2.5 × 230 cm [1" × 90½"]
Heavyweight fusible interfacing (lower gusset) - 60 × 10 cm [23⅝" × 4"]
Fusible interfacing (upper gusset, bag back) - 40 × 30 cm [15¾" × 11¾"]
1 Zipper - 38 cm [15"] long
Handles (leather or faux-leather) - 1 pair
2 Buttons (zipper pull) - 1.8 cm [⅝"]
1 Button (pocket front) - 1.3 cm [½"]
Embroidery floss - colors to match

Directions

1 Cut out the pattern pieces including the lining, facing, batting and fusible interfacing if called for.
2 Appliqué and embroider the design to the pocket front background piece. With wrong sides together, layer the appliquéd pocket front and the pocket lining with batting in between; baste and quilt. Bind the top edge of the pocket with the lt green bias binding.
3 With wrong sides together, layer the bag front and the bag front lining with batting in between; baste and quilt. Lay the pocket with right side out against the right side of the bag front; baste around the edges. Finding the center, vertically stitch the center of the pocket to the bag front from the lining side using a backstitch.
4 Fuse the interfacing to the wrong sides of the upper zipper and lower gussets and bag back. With wrong sides together, layer the gusset pieces with batting in between; baste and quilt. Repeat for the bag back.
5 Sew the zipper to the upper zipper gusset pieces; top stitch along the zipper edges; blindstitch the zipper tape down to the lining.
6 With right sides together, sew the upper zipper gusset to the lower gusset. Trim the excess seam allowances except for the lining. Use the lining to bind the raw edges; blindstitch down.
7 With right sides together, pin the bag front and bag back to the gusset, centering zipper and matching star marks. align the bias binding around the edges; pin and sew. Trim the seam allowances and bind the edges; blindstitch down.
8. Make the zipper pull and attach to the zipper clasp; sew the button to the top of the pocket to finish.

Dimensional Diagram

Bag Front

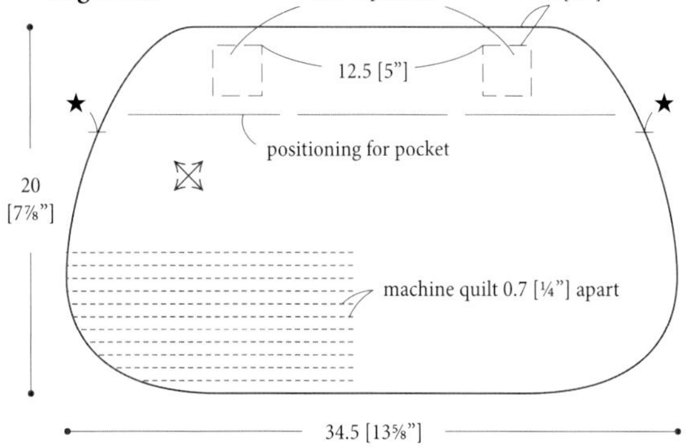
handle position
1 [⅜"]
12.5 [5"]
positioning for pocket
20 [7⅞"]
machine quilt 0.7 [¼"] apart
34.5 [13⅝"]

Bag Back

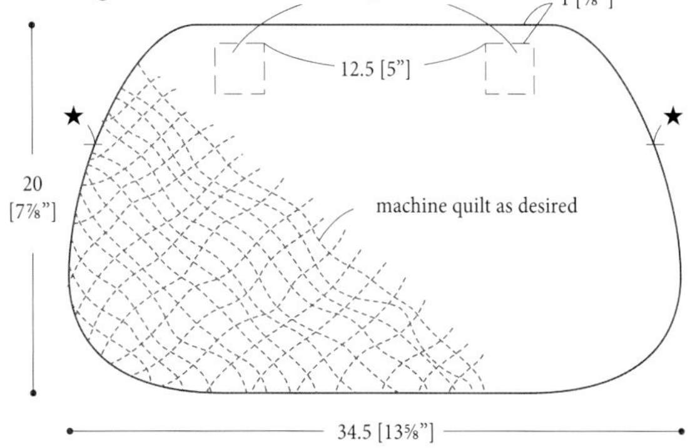
handle position
1 [⅜"]
12.5 [5"]
20 [7⅞"]
machine quilt as desired
34.5 [13⅝"]

Pocket

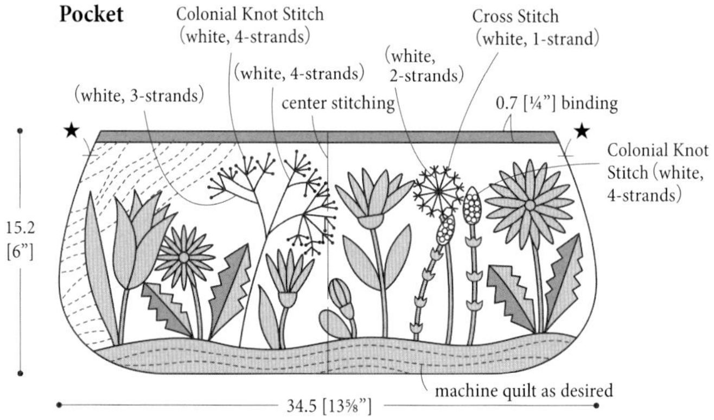
Colonial Knot Stitch (white, 4-strands)
Cross Stitch (white, 1-strand)
(white, 2-strands)
(white, 4-strands)
(white, 3-strands)
center stitching
0.7 [¼"] binding
Colonial Knot Stitch (white, 4-strands)
15.2 [6"]
machine quilt as desired
34.5 [13⅝"]

* outline quilt around each of the appliqués
* use an outline stitch for any area not specified

Upper Zipper Gusset

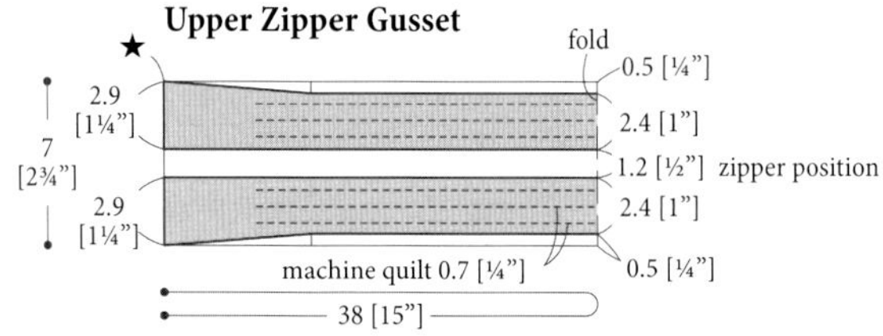
fold
0.5 [¼"]
2.9 [1¼"]
2.4 [1"]
7 [2¾"]
1.2 [½"] zipper position
2.9 [1¼"]
2.4 [1"]
machine quilt 0.7 [¼"]
0.5 [¼"]
38 [15"]

Lower Gusset

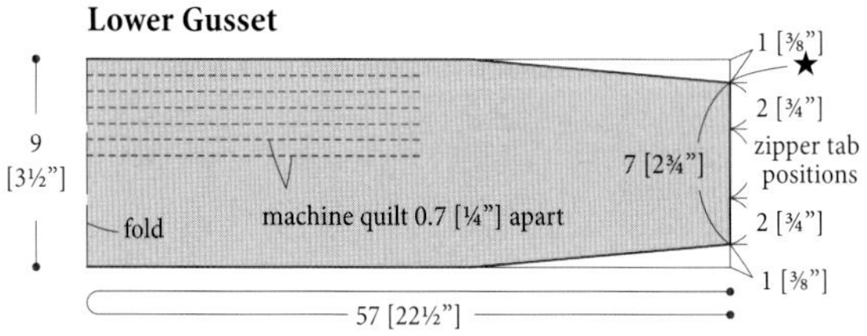
1 [⅜"]
2 [¾"]
zipper tab positions
9 [3½"]
7 [2¾"]
fold
machine quilt 0.7 [¼"] apart
2 [¾"]
1 [⅜"]
57 [22½"]

Bag Front

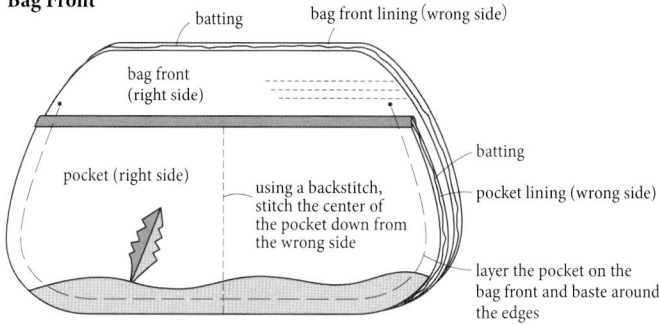

batting
bag front lining (wrong side)
bag front (right side)
pocket (right side)
batting
pocket lining (wrong side)
using a backstitch, stitch the center of the pocket down from the wrong side
layer the pocket on the bag front and baste around the edges

Bag Back

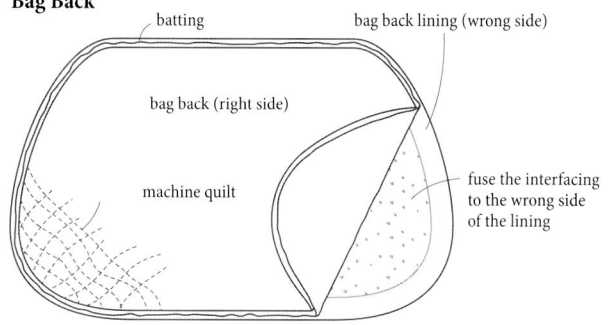

batting
bag back lining (wrong side)
bag back (right side)
machine quilt
fuse the interfacing to the wrong side of the lining

Upper Zipper Gusset

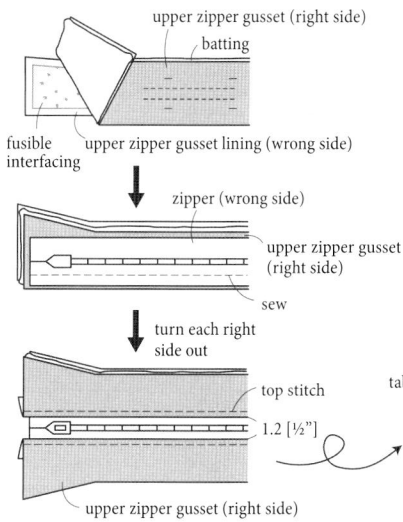

upper zipper gusset (right side)
batting
fusible interfacing
upper zipper gusset lining (wrong side)
zipper (wrong side)
upper zipper gusset (right side)
sew
turn each right side out
top stitch
1.2 [½"]
upper zipper gusset (right side)

Lower Gusset

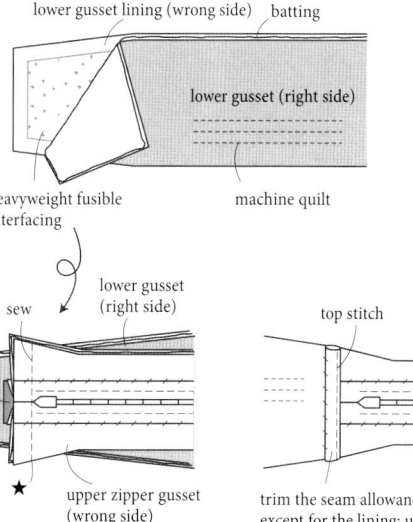

lower gusset lining (wrong side)
batting
lower gusset (right side)
heavyweight fusible interfacing
machine quilt
sew
lower gusset (right side)
tab
upper zipper gusset (wrong side)
★
top stitch
trim the seam allowances of all layers except for the lining; use it to bind the raw edges; blindstitch down

Zipper Tabs - cut 2

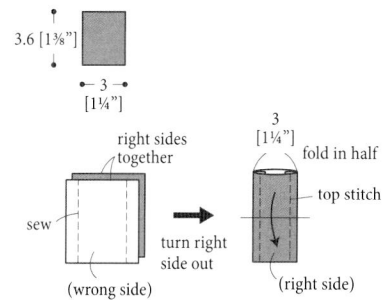

3.6 [1⅜"]
3 [1¼"]
right sides together
sew
(wrong side)
turn right side out
3 [1¼"]
fold in half
top stitch
(right side)

Sewing the Bag Together

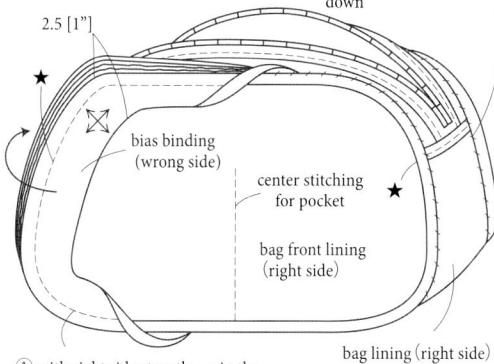

2.5 [1"]
★
bias binding (wrong side)
center stitching for pocket
bag front lining (right side)
★
bag lining (right side)
① with right sides together, pin the sewn-together gusset and bag front and bag back together; align the bias binding to the edges; sew around both sides
② trim the seam allowances of all layers; use bias binding to bind the raw edges; blindstitch down

Zipper Pull

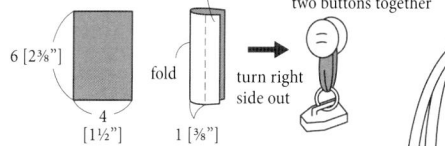

6 [2⅜"]
4 [1½"]
fold
1 [⅜"]
(wrong side)
turn right side out
slip through zipper clasp; secure by sewing two buttons together

Attaching the Handles

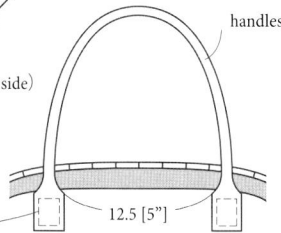

handles
12.5 [5"]
stitch the handles securely in place with two strands of hand-sewing thread, following the pre-punched holes

Completed Bag

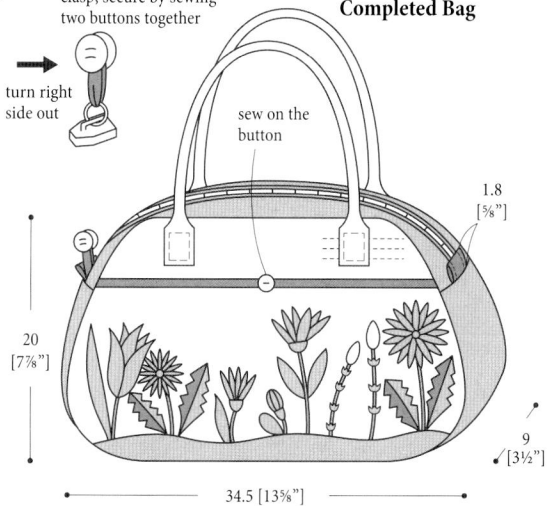

sew on the button
1.8 [⅝"]
20 [7⅞"]
9 [3½"]
34.5 [13⅝"]

shown on p. 10

4 Berries & Branches Shoulder Bag

The template/pattern can be found on Side A of the pattern sheet inserts.

Materials

Assorted fat quarters or scraps (appliqué)
Grey print (pocket) - 40×40 cm [15¾" × 15¾"]
Lt green homespun (bag front) - 45×40 cm
  [17¾" × 15¾"]
Grey print (bag back) - 45×40 cm [17¾" × 15¾"]
Beige homespun (gusset) - 110×10 cm [43¼" × 4"]
Homespun (lining) - 100×100 cm [39⅜" × 39⅜"]
Batting - 100×100 cm [39⅜" × 39⅜"]
Beige dot (bias binding) - 3.5×280 cm [1⅜"×110¼"]
Heavyweight fusible interfacing - 100×40 cm
  [39⅜" × 15¾"]
Woven webbing (strap) - 4×150 cm [1½"×59"]
2 Rectangle rings (strap hardware) - 4 cm [1½"]
1 Double ring (strap hardware) - 4 cm [1½"]
Embroidery floss - colors to match

Directions

1 Cut out the pattern pieces including the lining, facing, batting and fusible interfacing if called for.
2 Appliqué, piece and embroider the design to the pocket. With wrong sides together, layer the appliquéd pocket front and the pocket lining with batting in between; baste and quilt. Bind the top edge of the pocket with the bias binding.
3 Fuse the interfacing pieces to the bag back and gusset. For the bag front, bag back and gusset, with wrong sides together, layer them with the matching linings with batting in between; baste and quilt.
4 Bind the top edges of the bag front and bag back. Lay the pocket on top of the bag front; baste around the edges.
5 With wrong sides together, align the gusset to the bag front and back; baste. Pin the bias binding around the seams; sew. Trim the seam allowances; blindstitch the binding down toward the gusset.
6 Make the tabs; slip them through the rectangle rings.
7 Make the shoulder strap using the woven webbing and the hardware following the diagram. Sew the shoulder strap to the hardware; sew to the tops of the gussets to finish.

Dimensional Diagram

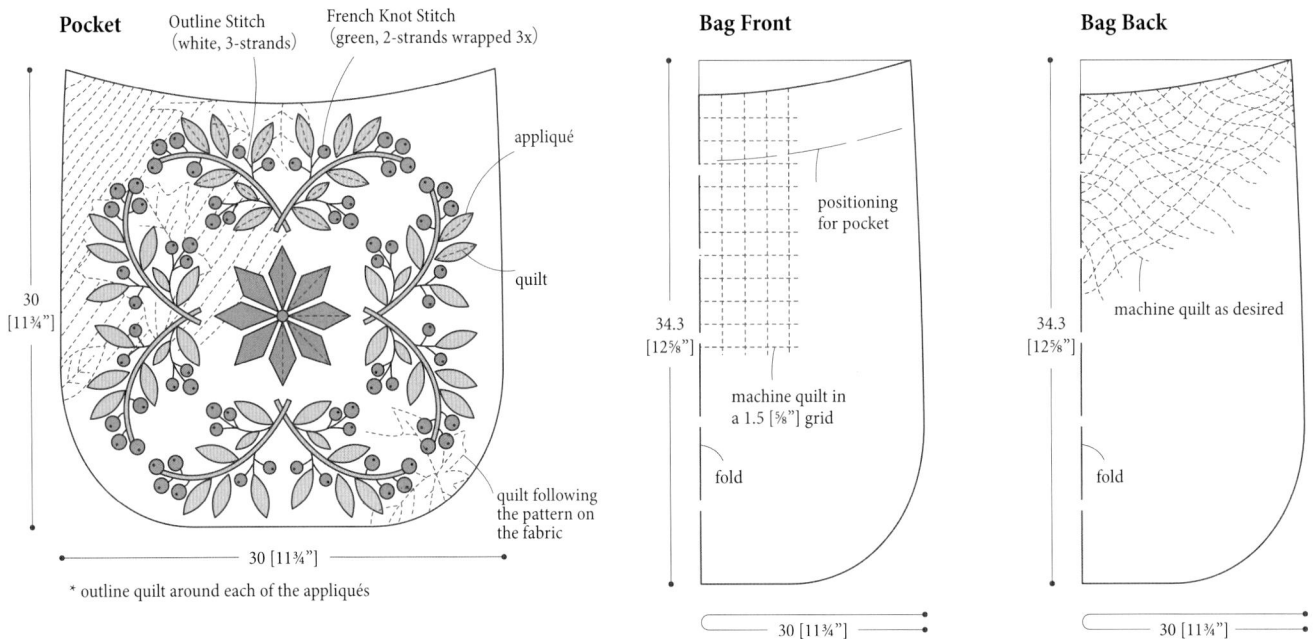

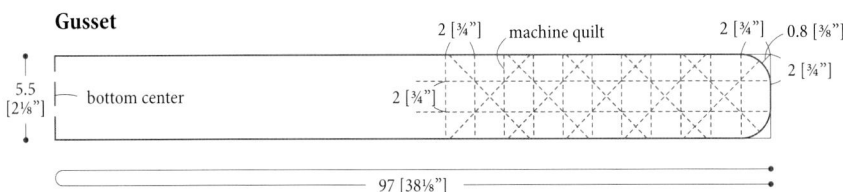

Pocket

Outline Stitch (white, 3-strands)
French Knot Stitch (green, 2-strands wrapped 3x)

appliqué

quilt

quilt following the pattern on the fabric

30 [11¾"]

30 [11¾"]

* outline quilt around each of the appliqués

Bag Front

positioning for pocket

34.3 [12⅝"]

machine quilt in a 1.5 [⅝"] grid

fold

30 [11¾"]

Bag Back

machine quilt as desired

34.3 [12⅝"]

fold

30 [11¾"]

Gusset

5.5 [2⅛"]

bottom center

2 [¾"] machine quilt 2 [¾"] 0.8 [⅜"]

2 [¾"]

2 [¾"]

97 [38⅛"]

French Knot Stitch

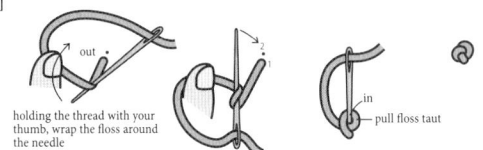

out

holding the thread with your thumb, wrap the floss around the needle

in

pull floss taut

Pocket

3.5 [1⅜"]

sew

0.7 [¼"] binding

bias binding (wrong side)

quilt

appliqué

batting

pocket lining (wrong side)

pocket (right side)

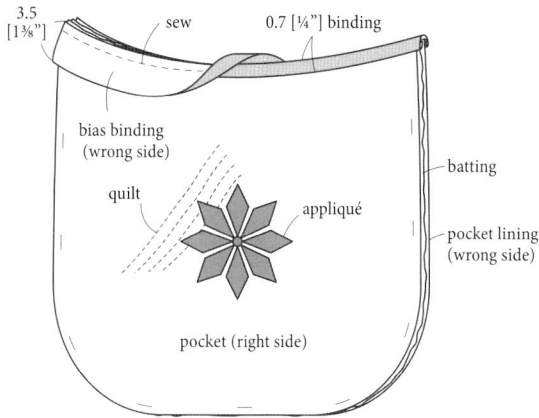

* using the bag front pattern, make the bag front in the same way as the bag back and pocket (without the appliqué); quilt in a grid pattern

Bag Back

3.5 [1⅜"]

sew

0.7 [¼"] binding

machine quilt

bias binding (wrong side)

bag back (right side)

batting

bag back lining (wrong side)

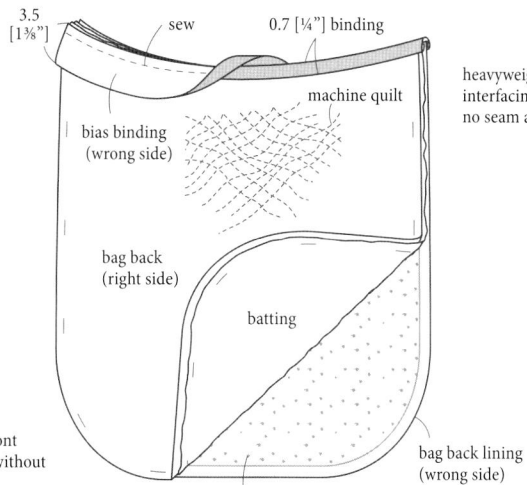

heavyweight fusible interfacing (cut with no seam allowance)

Gusset

gusset lining (wrong side)

heavyweight fusible interfacing (cut with no seam allowance)

batting

gusset (right side)

machine quilt

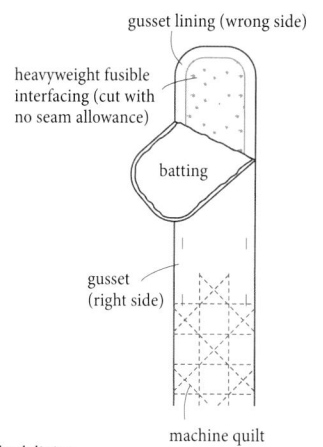

Sewing the Bag Together

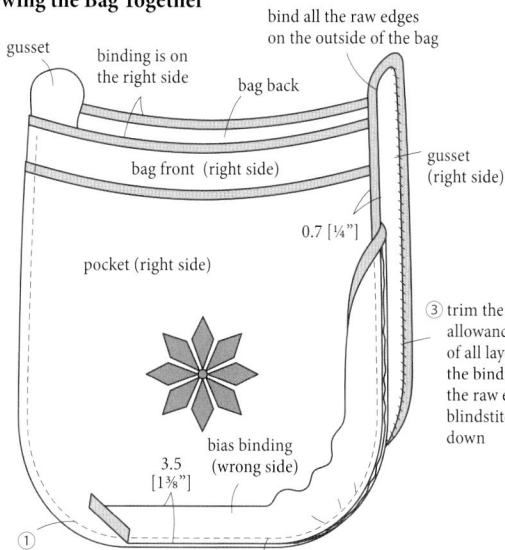

gusset

binding is on the right side

bind all the raw edges on the outside of the bag

bag back

bag front (right side)

gusset (right side)

0.7 [¼"]

pocket (right side)

③ trim the seam allowances of all layers; use the binding to bind the raw edges; blindstitch down

3.5 [1⅜"]

bias binding (wrong side)

①

② sew

with wrong sides together, pin the sewn-together gusset and bag front and bag back together; align the bias binding to the edges; sew around both sides

Attaching the Metal Hardware and Tabs to the Gusset

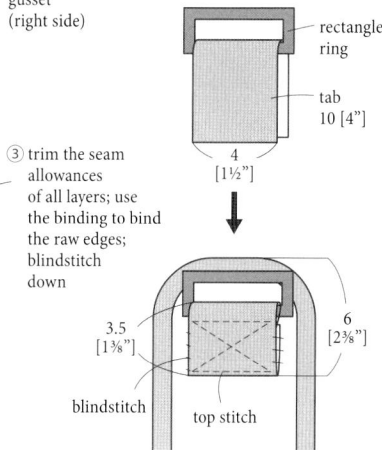

rectangle ring

tab 10 [4"]

4 [1½"]

3.5 [1⅜"]

6 [2⅜"]

blindstitch

top stitch

Completed Bag

38.7 [15⅛"]

6.9 [2¾"]

31.4 [12⅜"]

Making the Shoulder Strap

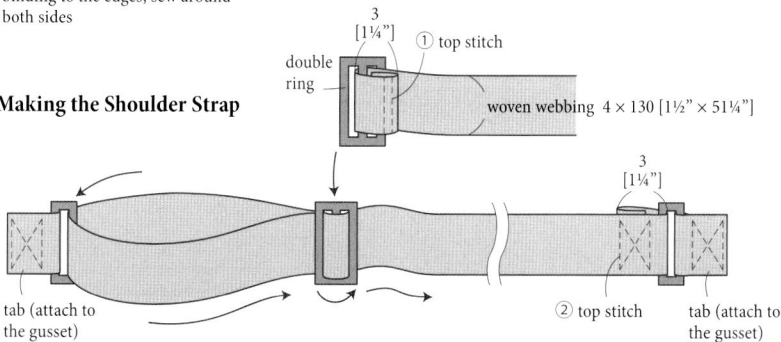

3 [1¼"]

① top stitch

double ring

woven webbing 4 × 130 [1½" × 51¼"]

3 [1¼"]

tab (attach to the gusset)

② top stitch

tab (attach to the gusset)

shown on p. 12

5 Floral Star Handbag

> The template/pattern can be found on Side A of the pattern sheet inserts.

Materials

Assorted fat quarters or scraps (patchwork, appliqué)
Beige print (bag back) - 35 × 35 cm [13¾" × 13¾"]
Beige dot print (gusset) - 25 × 30 cm [9¾" × 11¾"]
Beige print (bottom) - 25 × 15 cm[9¾" × 5⅞"]
Beige print (lining) - 100 × 50 cm [39⅜" × 19¾"]
Batting - 100 × 50 cm [39⅜" × 19¾"]
Beige check (bias binding) - 3.5 × 80 cm[1⅜" × 31½"]
Heavyweight fusible interfacing (bottom) - 20 × 10 cm
    [7⅞" × 4"]
Med-weight fusible interfacing - 55 × 35 cm
    [21⅝" × 13¾"]
1 Zipper - 30 cm [11¾"] long
Handles (leather or faux-leather) - 1 pair
2 Beads (zipper pull)
Waxed cord (zipper pull)
MOCO* variegated floss (grey)
Embroidery floss - colors to match

* MOCO is a brand of variegated embroidery floss

Directions

1 Cut out the pattern pieces including the lining, facing, batting and fusible interfacing if called for.
2 Piece together the bag front from assorted fabric. Appliqué, piece and embroider the design to the bag front. With right sides together, layer the bag front lining and the appliquéd bag front on top of the batting; sew the sides and the bottom seams. Turn right side out; quilt.
3 Fuse the interfacing to the bag back lining (do not do this for the bag front), the gusset and bag bottom. With right sides together, layer the bag back lining and the bag back on top of the batting; sew the sides and the bottom seams. Turn right side out; quilt.
4 Repeat for the gusset and bag bottom, leaving the ends open as shown for turning. Turn right side out; blindstitch the openings closed; quilt.
5 With wrong sides together, whipstitch the bag bottom to the bottom edges of the bag front and bag back. Pin the gussets to each side; whipstitch the gussets to the sides of the bag back and bag front. Pinching the seams, sew a Running Stitch along all the seams using the MOCO variegated floss.
6 Using a backstitch, sew the zipper to the lining of the bag front and bag back aligning the edges; bind the top edges and blindstitch down to the zipper tape.
7 Sew on the handles. Make and attach the zipper pull to finish.

Dimensional Diagram * use an outline stitch for any area not specified

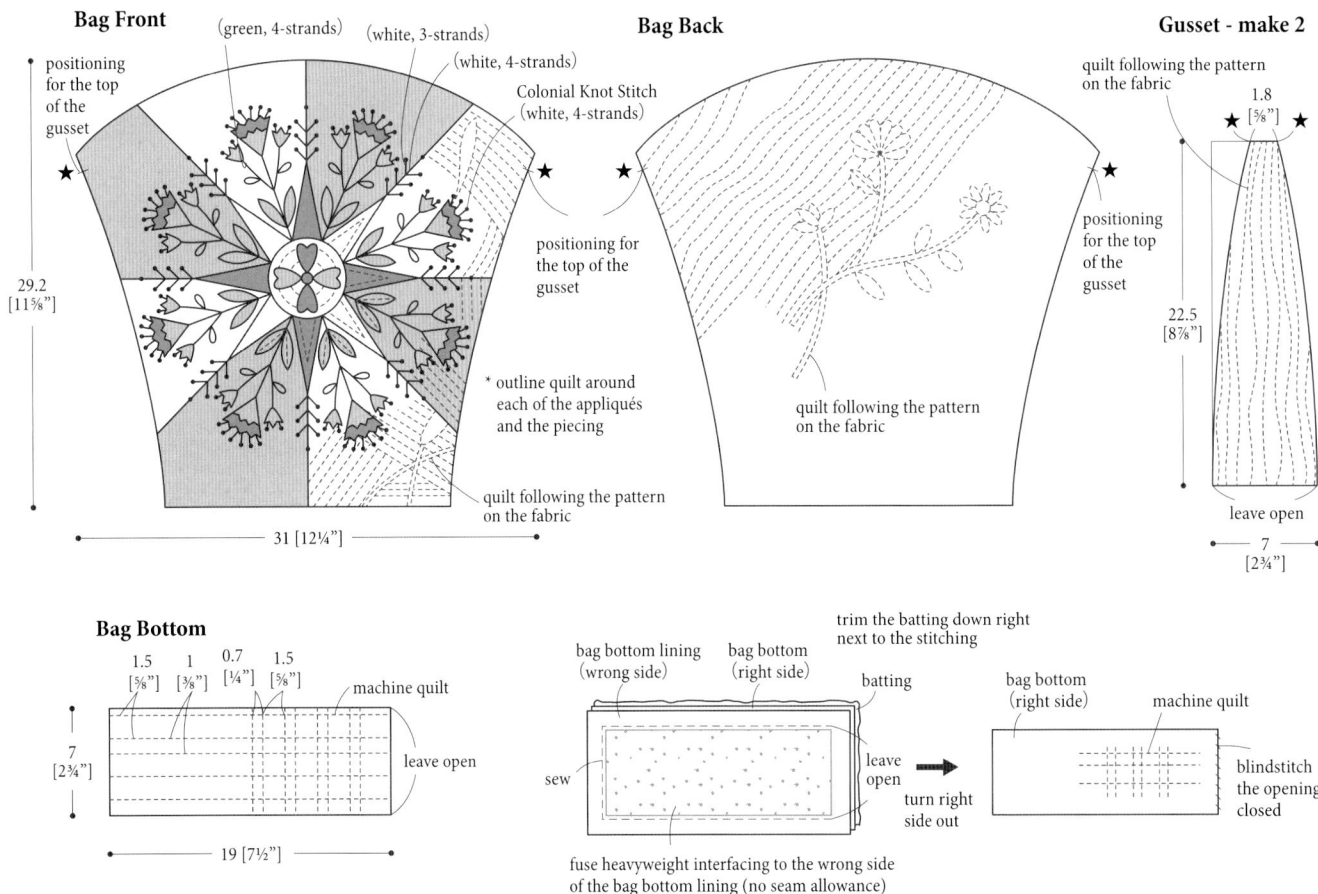

Bag Front

(green, 4-strands)
(white, 3-strands)
(white, 4-strands)
Colonial Knot Stitch (white, 4-strands)

positioning for the top of the gusset

29.2 [11⅝"]

31 [12¼"]

* outline quilt around each of the appliqués and the piecing

quilt following the pattern on the fabric

Bag Back

positioning for the top of the gusset

quilt following the pattern on the fabric

Gusset - make 2

quilt following the pattern on the fabric

1.8 [⅝"]

positioning for the top of the gusset

22.5 [8⅞"]

leave open

7 [2¾"]

Bag Bottom

1.5 [⅝"] 1 [⅜"] 0.7 [¼"] 1.5 [⅝"]

machine quilt

leave open

7 [2¾"]

19 [7½"]

trim the batting down right next to the stitching

bag bottom lining (wrong side)
bag bottom (right side)
batting

sew

leave open

fuse heavyweight interfacing to the wrong side of the bag bottom lining (no seam allowance)

turn right side out

bag bottom (right side)
machine quilt

blindstitch the opening closed

Bag Back

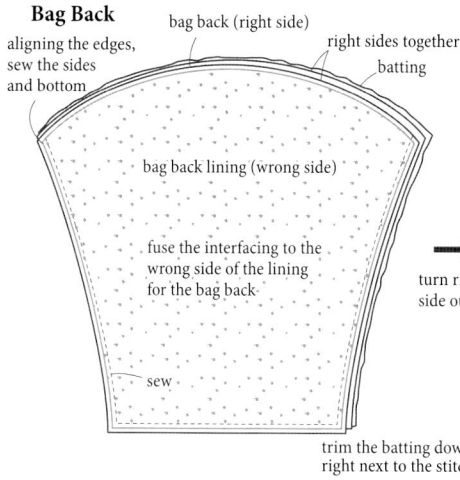

aligning the edges, sew the sides and bottom

bag back (right side)

right sides together

batting

bag back lining (wrong side)

fuse the interfacing to the wrong side of the lining for the bag back

sew

trim the batting down right next to the stitching

turn right side out

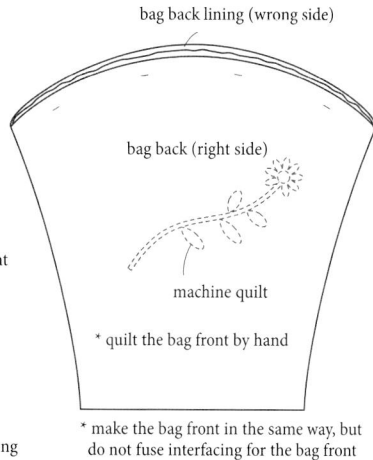

bag back lining (wrong side)

bag back (right side)

machine quilt

* quilt the bag front by hand

* make the bag front in the same way, but do not fuse interfacing for the bag front

Gusset

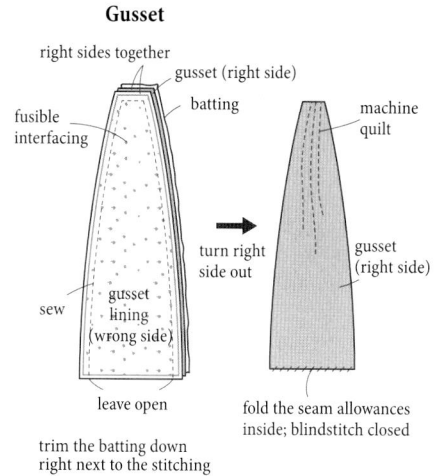

right sides together

gusset (right side)

batting

fusible interfacing

sew

gusset lining (wrong side)

leave open

trim the batting down right next to the stitching

turn right side out

machine quilt

gusset (right side)

fold the seam allowances inside; blindstitch closed

Sewing the Bag Together

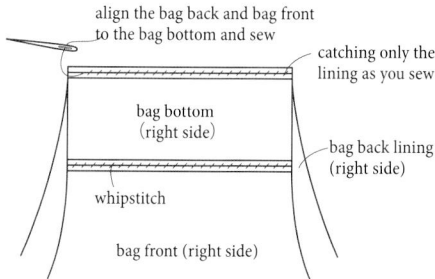

align the bag back and bag front to the bag bottom and sew

catching only the lining as you sew

bag bottom (right side)

bag back lining (right side)

whipstitch

bag front (right side)

Sewing the Gusset to the Bag

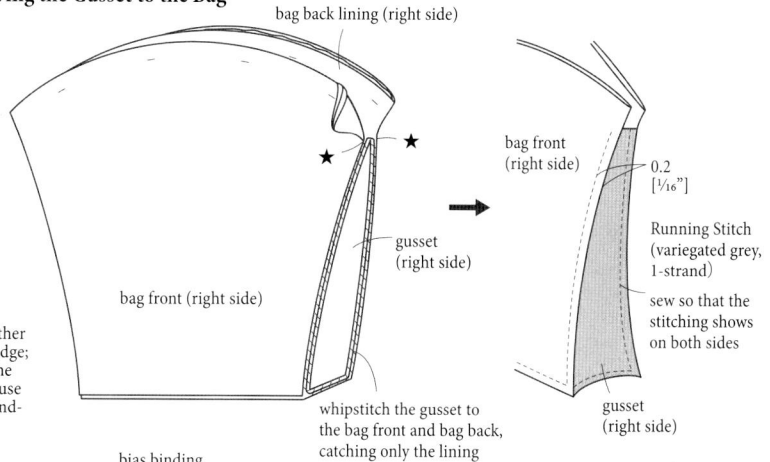

bag back lining (right side)

★ ★

bag front (right side)

gusset (right side)

whipstitch the gusset to the bag front and bag back, catching only the lining

bag front (right side)

0.2 [1/16"]

Running Stitch (variegated grey, 1-strand)

sew so that the stitching shows on both sides

gusset (right side)

Sewing in the Zipper

layer the binding with right sides together against the top of the zipper opening edge; lay the zipper with right side against the wrong side of the binding; stitch; flip; use the binding to cover raw edges and blind-stitch down

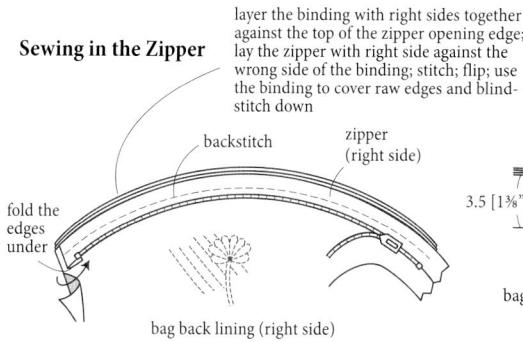

backstitch

zipper (right side)

fold the edges under

bag back lining (right side)

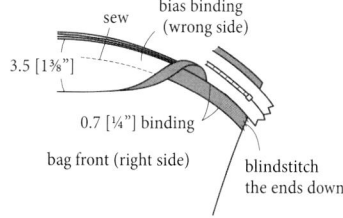

sew

bias binding (wrong side)

3.5 [1⅜"]

0.7 [¼"] binding

bag front (right side)

blindstitch the ends down

Completed Bag

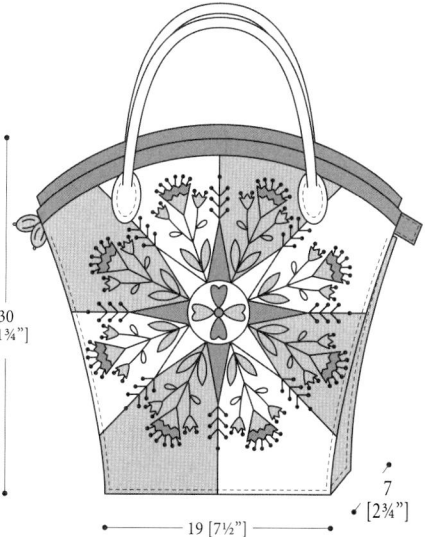

30 [11¾"]

19 [7½"]

7 [2¾"]

Zipper Pull

cut

cord

blindstitch

beads

leaving a tail, make a knot to secure; feed the tail back through the bead; cut

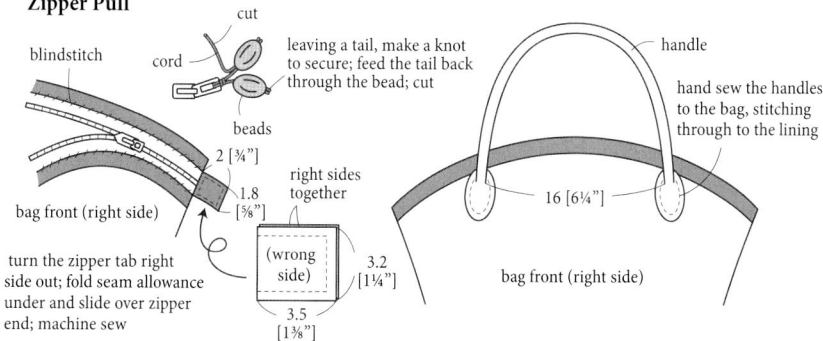

2 [¾"]

1.8 [⅝"]

bag front (right side)

right sides together

(wrong side)

3.2 [1¼"]

3.5 [1⅜"]

turn the zipper tab right side out; fold seam allowance under and slide over zipper end; machine sew

handle

hand sew the handles to the bag, stitching through to the lining

16 [6¼"]

bag front (right side)

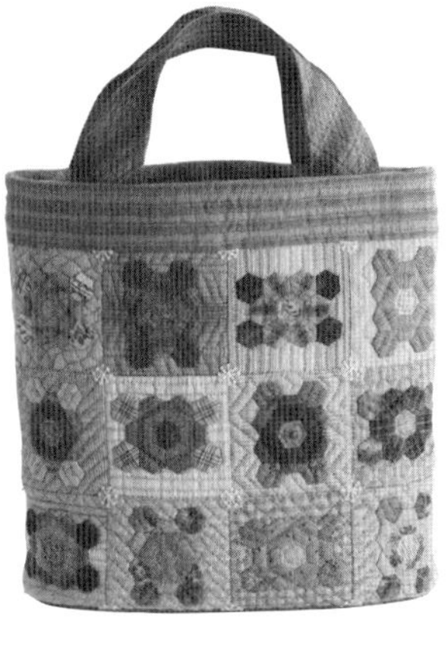

shown on p. 14

6 Grandmother's Flower Garden Tote

The template/pattern can be found on Side A of the pattern sheet inserts.

Materials

Assorted fat quarters or scraps (piecing including bag opening border; appliqué)
Brown plaid (bottom) - 15 × 35 cm [5⅞" × 13¾"]
Brown plaid (handles) - 35 × 50 cm [13¾" × 19¾"]
Homespun (lining) - 110 × 50 cm [43¼" × 19¾"]
Batting - 110 × 50 cm [43¼" × 19¾"]
Homespun (bias binding for seam allowances) - 2.5 × 75 cm [1" × 29½"]
Heavyweight fusible interfacing (bottom facing) - 30 × 15 cm [11¾" × 5⅞"]
Med-weight fusible interfacing (bottom) - 30 × 15 cm [11¾" × 5⅞"]
MOCO* variegated floss - colors to match

* MOCO is a brand of variegated embroidery floss

Directions

1 Cut out the pattern pieces including the lining, facing, batting and fusible interfacing if called for.
2 Appliqué, piece and embroider the design for the bag front and bag back.
3 Cut the bag front and bag back linings and batting slightly bigger than the bag front and bag back. With wrong sides together, layer the bag front and bag front lining with batting in between; baste; quilt. Repeat for the bag back. With right sides together, sew the bag front and bag back together. Bind the edges with the lining fabric following the diagram.
4 Fuse the interfacing to the wrong side of the bag bottom facing and the bag bottom lining. With wrong sides together, layer the bag bottom and bag bottom facing with batting in between; baste; machine quilt.
5 With right sides together, backstitch the bag bottom to the bag body, with facing side out. Lay the bag bottom lining over the facing covering the bag bottom seams; blindstitch down.
6 With right sides together, layer the handle and handle lining with batting in between; baste; quilt. Pin the handles to the right side of the bag body in position; align the bias binding along the bag opening edge sandwiching the handles; sew. Trim the handle ends even with the edge, bind the bag opening edge; blindstitch to the lining.
7 Embroider the design along the side seams to match the rest of the bag body to finish.

Dimensional Diagram

Bag Front & Bag Back (make 1 each)

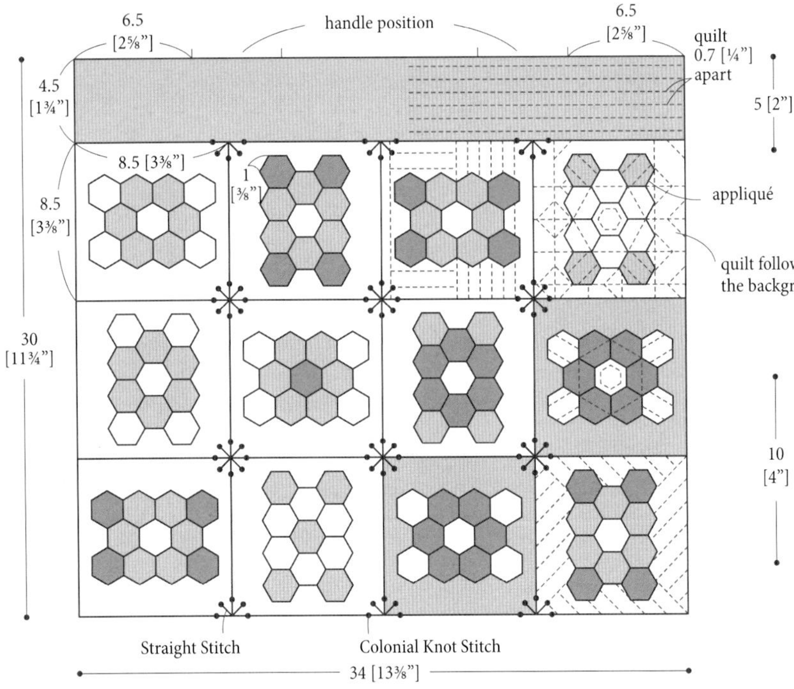
6.5 [2⅝"]
handle position
6.5 [2⅝"]
quilt 0.7 [¼"] apart
4.5 [1¾"]
8.5 [3⅜"]
1 [⅜"]
8.5 [3⅜"]
30 [11¾"]
appliqué
quilt following the patterns of the background fabric for each block
Straight Stitch
Colonial Knot Stitch
34 [13⅜"]

Handles - make 2

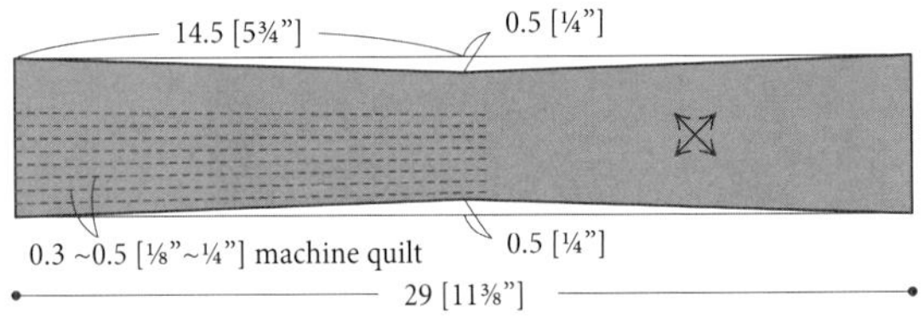
14.5 [5¾"]
0.5 [¼"]
5 [2"]
0.3 ~0.5 [⅛"~¼"] machine quilt
0.5 [¼"]
29 [11⅜"]

Bag Bottom (make a little large, cut to size after quilting)

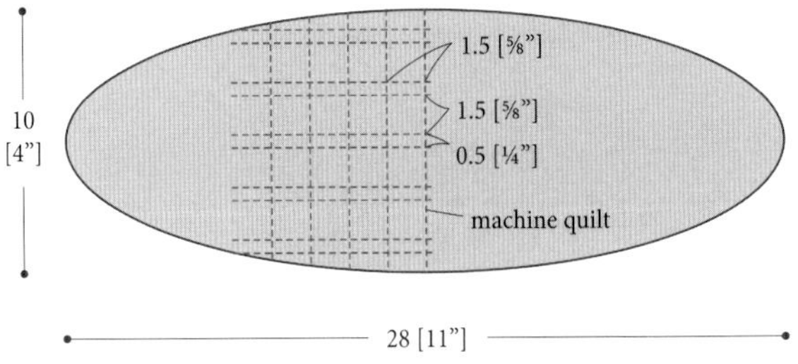
1.5 [⅝"]
1.5 [⅝"]
0.5 [¼"]
10 [4"]
machine quilt
28 [11"]

* outline quilt around the piecing and each of the appliqués
* use a variegated embroidery floss for all stitches

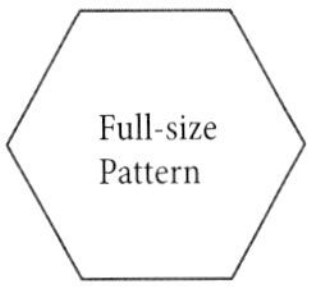
Full-size Pattern

Straight Stitch

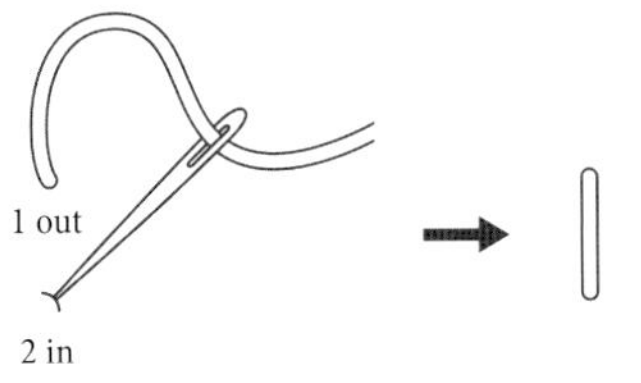
1 out
2 in

Making the Bag Front and Back

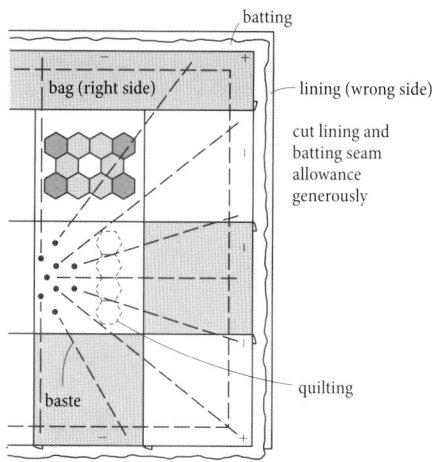

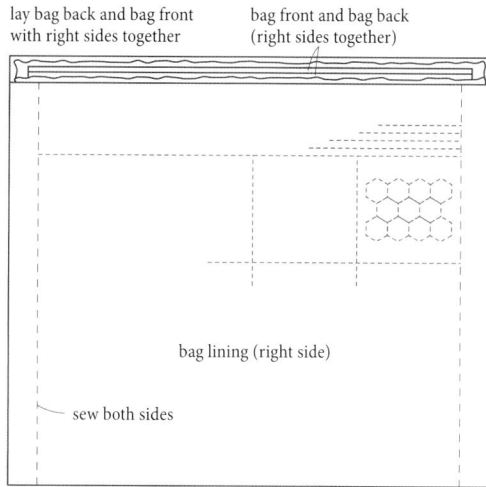

batting

bag (right side)

lining (wrong side)

cut lining and batting seam allowance generously

quilting

baste

lay bag back and bag front with right sides together

bag front and bag back (right sides together)

bag lining (right side)

sew both sides

Binding the Edges

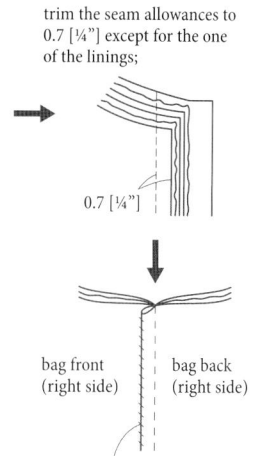

trim the seam allowances to 0.7 [¼"] except for the one of the linings;

0.7 [¼"]

bag front (right side)

bag back (right side)

use the lining to bind the raw edges; blindstitch down to the lining

Making the Bag Bottom

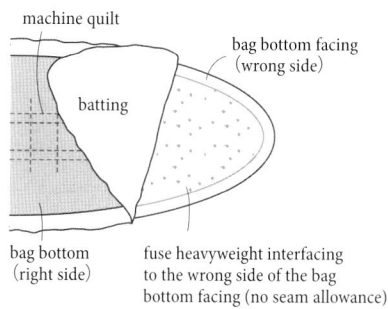

machine quilt

bag bottom facing (wrong side)

batting

bag bottom (right side)

fuse heavyweight interfacing to the wrong side of the bag bottom facing (no seam allowance)

with right sides together align the bag bottom and the bag body; sew together

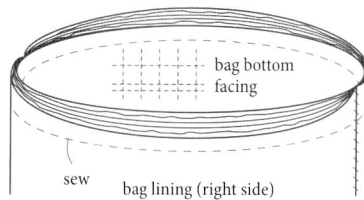

bag bottom facing

sew

bag lining (right side)

med-weight fusible interfacing (no seam allowance)

② spray adhesive to the bag bottom facing; with wrong sides together, lay bag bottom lining with interfacing down; blindstitch to the bag body lining

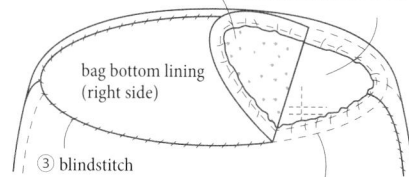

bag bottom lining (right side)

③ blindstitch

bag lining (right side)

① backstitch the seam allowance down to the bag bottom

Making the Handles

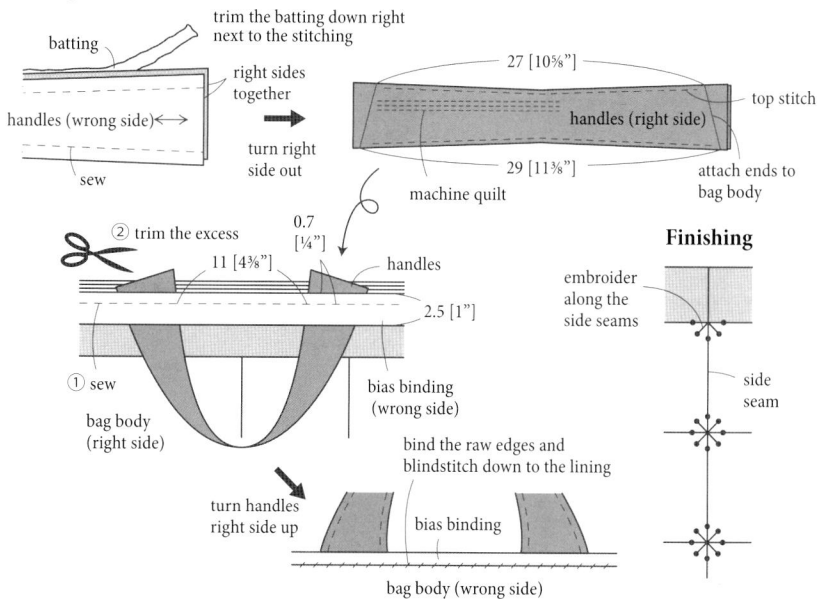

batting

trim the batting down right next to the stitching

right sides together

handles (wrong side)

sew

turn right side out

27 [10⅝"]

handles (right side)

top stitch

29 [11⅜"]

machine quilt

attach ends to bag body

0.7 [¼"]

② trim the excess

11 [4⅜"]

handles

2.5 [1"]

① sew

bag body (right side)

bias binding (wrong side)

turn handles right side up

bias binding

bind the raw edges and blindstitch down to the lining

bag body (wrong side)

Finishing

embroider along the side seams

side seam

Completed Tote

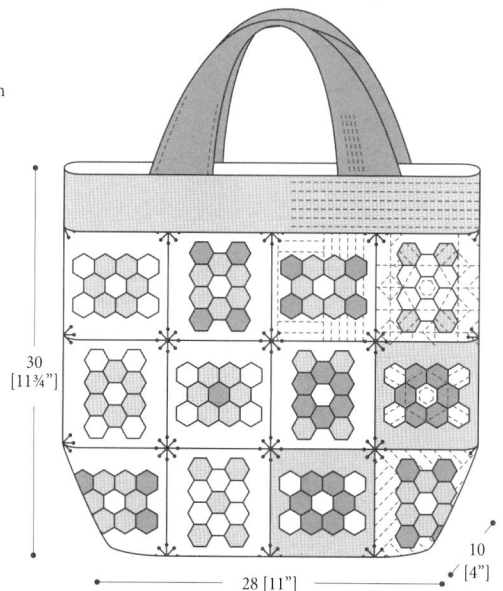

30 [11¾"]

28 [11"]

10 [4"]

shown on p. 16

7 Lovers Mini-Pouch with Handles

The template/pattern can be found on Side B of the pattern sheet inserts.

Materials

Assorted fat quarters or scraps (appliqué)
Black check (gusset) - 50×15 cm [19¾" × 5⅞"]
Black dot (pockets) - 20×55 cm [7⅞" × 21⅝"]
Homespun (lining) - 55×50 cm [21⅝" × 19¾"]
Batting - 55×50 cm [21⅝" × 19¾"]
Homespun (bias binding for seam allowances) -
    2.5×120 cm [1"×47¼"]
Fusible interfacing - 15×50 cm [5⅞" × 19¾"]
1 Zipper - 30 cm [11¾"] long
Handles (leather or faux-leather) - 1 pair
1 Bead (zipper pull)
Jump ring (zipper pull)
Embroidery floss - colors to match

Directions

1 Cut out the pattern pieces including the lining, facing, batting and fusible interfacing if called for.
2 Appliqué, piece and embroider the design for the pouch front section. With wrong sides together and batting in between, layer the pouch body and pouch body lining; baste and quilt.
3 Fuse the interfacing to the wrong side of the gusset lining. With wrong sides together, layer the gusset and gusset lining with batting in between. Lay the zipper facing with the right sides together in the center of the gusset; stitch along the guidelines as shown; carefully cut a slit down the center between the stitching; turn the zipper facing inside out to the gusset lining. Turn the edges under; blindstitch to the gusset lining.
4 Lay the right side of the zipper against the zipper facing, aligning centers, and backstitch next to the zipper teeth to the facing. Blindstitch the edges down. Turn over; quilt the gusset and top stitch around the zipper.
5 Make the pockets following the diagrams; align to the two ends of the gusset on the right side; sew around the edges.
6 Baste the handles in place as shown. With right sides together, pin the gusset to the pouch body; sew the seams. Pin the bias binding around the seam allowances; sew. Trim the seam allowances; blindstitch the binding down to the lining.
7 Make and attach the zipper pull to finish.

Dimensional Diagram

Pouch Body

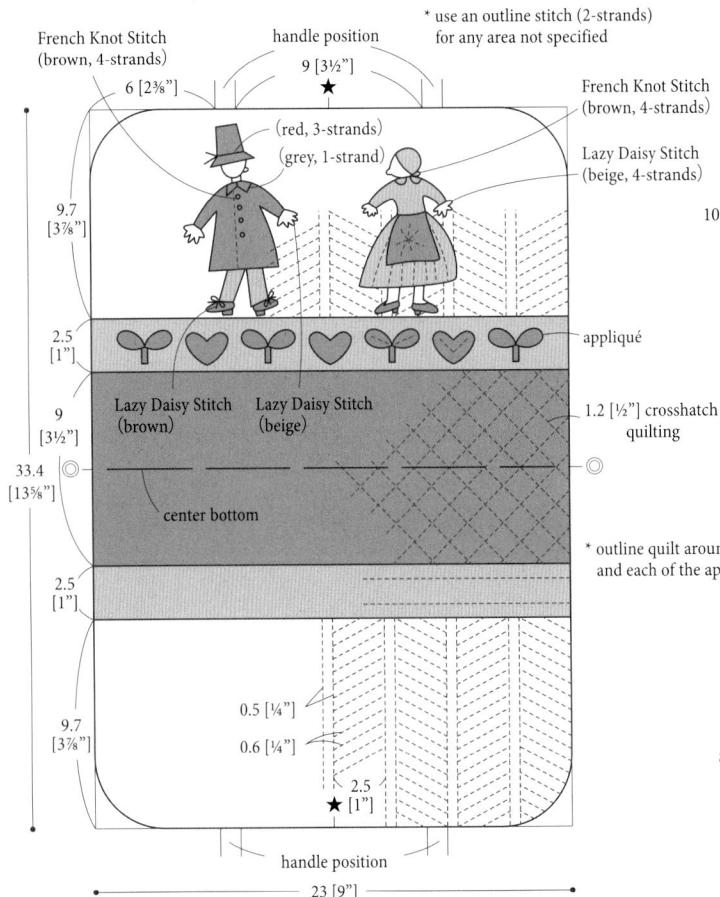

Gusset

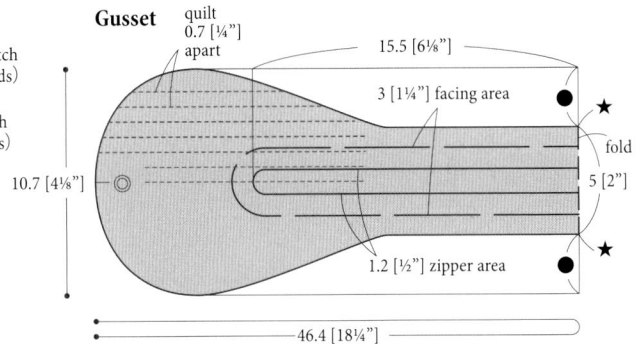

Zipper Facing

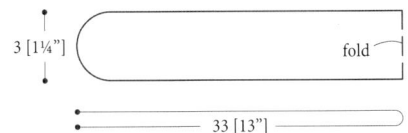

Pocket - make 2

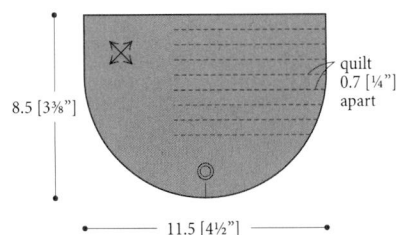

Pouch Body

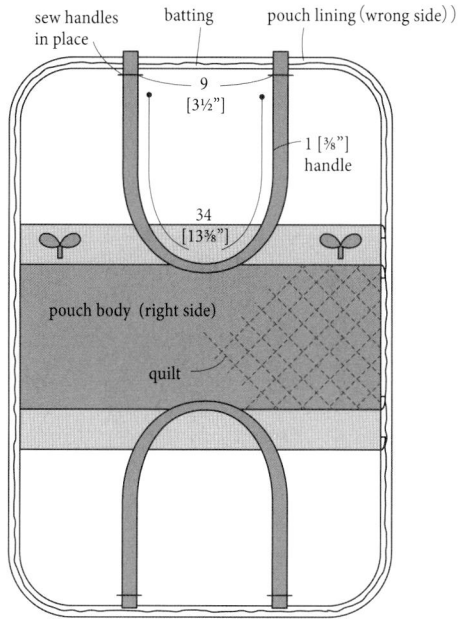

sew handles in place
batting
pouch lining (wrong side)

9 [3½"]

1 [⅜"] handle

34 [13⅜"]

pouch body (right side)

quilt

Pocket

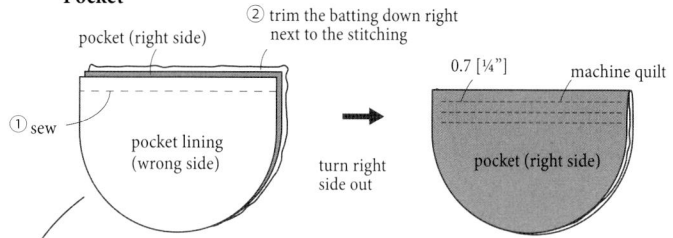

pocket (right side)

② trim the batting down right next to the stitching

① sew

pocket lining (wrong side)

turn right side out

0.7 [¼"]   machine quilt

pocket (right side)

Gusset

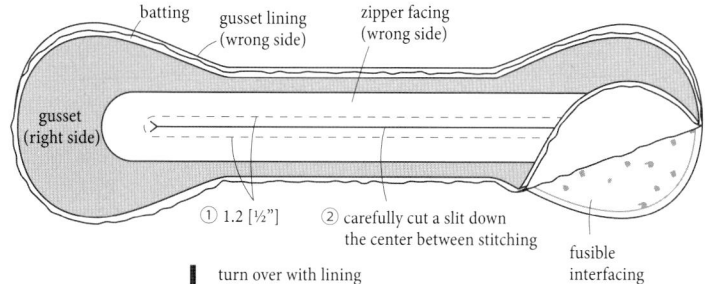

batting
gusset lining (wrong side)
zipper facing (wrong side)

gusset (right side)

① 1.2 [½"]

② carefully cut a slit down the center between stitching

fusible interfacing

turn over with lining side facing up

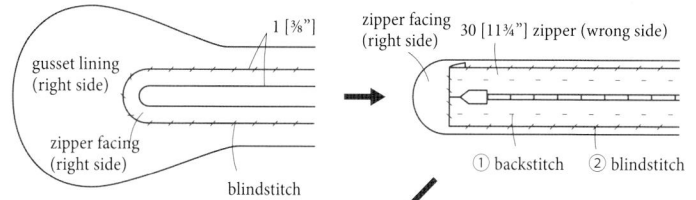

1 [⅜"]

gusset lining (right side)

zipper facing (right side)

blindstitch

zipper facing (right side)
30 [11¾"] zipper (wrong side)

① backstitch   ② blindstitch

Sewing the Pocket to the Gusset

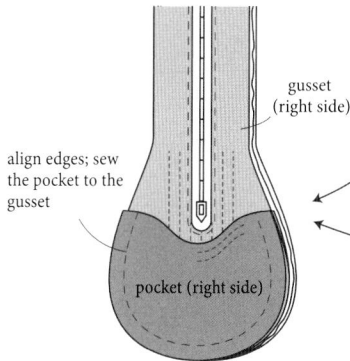

gusset (right side)

align edges; sew the pocket to the gusset

pocket (right side)

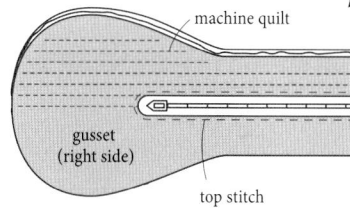

machine quilt

gusset (right side)

top stitch

Sewing the Pouch Together

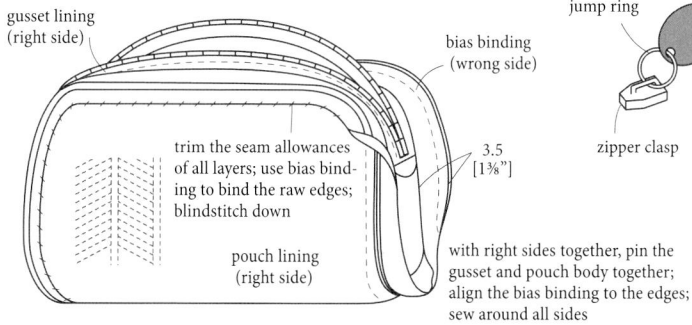

gusset lining (right side)

trim the seam allowances of all layers; use bias binding to bind the raw edges; blindstitch down

pouch lining (right side)

bias binding (wrong side)

3.5 [1⅜"]

with right sides together, pin the gusset and pouch body together; align the bias binding to the edges; sew around all sides

Zipper Pull

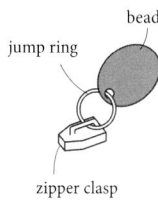

bead

jump ring

zipper clasp

Completed Pouch

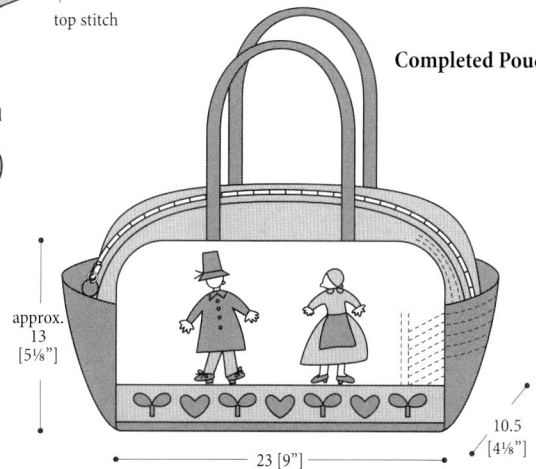

approx. 13 [5⅛"]

23 [9"]

10.5 [4⅛"]

shown on p. 18

8 Things We Love Bucket Bag

Materials

Assorted fat quarters or scraps (appliqué)
Beige homespun (bag body) - 30 × 70 cm
   [11¾" × 27½"]
Brown plaid (bottom, handle, bag body C)
   - 60 × 60 cm [23⅝" × 23⅝"]
Homespun (lining) - 100 × 50 cm [39⅜" × 19¾"]
Batting -100 × 50 cm [39⅜" × 19¾"]
Brown check (bias binding) - 3.5 × 60 cm [1⅜" × 23⅝"]
Heavyweight fusible interfacing (bottom) - 20 × 20 cm
   [7⅞" × 7⅞"]
Med-weight fusible interfacing - 20 × 55 cm
   [7⅞" × 21⅝"]
Embroidery floss - colors to match

Directions

1 Cut out the pattern pieces including the lining, facing, batting and fusible interfacing if called for.
2 Appliqué and embroider the design for bag body A and B. With wrong sides together, lay bag body A and bag body A lining with batting in between; baste; quilt. Repeat for bag body B.
3 With wrong sides together, lay bag body C and bag body C lining together with batting in between; baste; machine quilt and sew the darts. Make two.
4 With right sides together, sew bag body A and one bag body C together. Repeat for bag body B. Sew the side seams together. Trim the seams and use the linings to bind the seam allowances (see diagrams).
5 Fuse the interfacing to the wrong side of the bag bottom facing and the bag bottom lining. With wrong sides together, layer the bag bottom and bag bottom facing with batting in between; baste; machine quilt (see p. 83).
4. With right sides together, sew the bag bottom to the bag body, with facing side out. Lay the bag bottom lining over the facing covering the bag bottom seams; blindstitch down.
5 Fuse the interfacing to the wrong side of the handle lining. With right sides together, layer the handle lining and the handle on top of the batting; sew around the edges leaving an opening for turning. Turn right side out; machine quilt.
6 Align the ends of the handle in place against the bag lining inside and baste in place. With right sides together, align the bias binding around the bag opening; sew. Bind the seam allowance; blindstitch the binding down to the lining (and over the handle ends).
7 Pull handles up to finish.

Dimensional Diagram

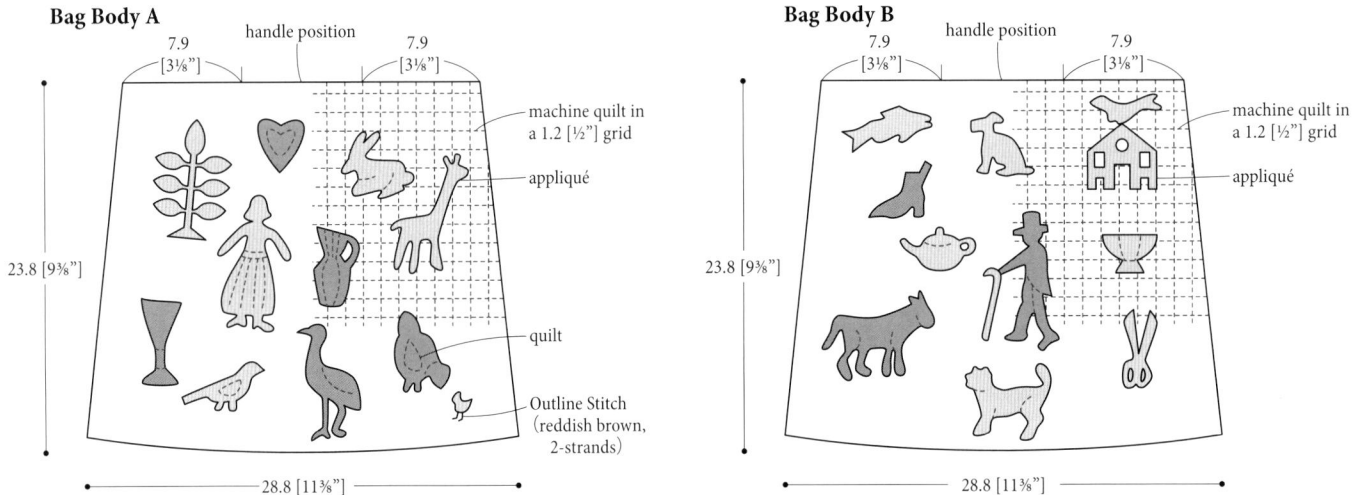

Bag Body A

7.9 [3⅛"]   handle position   7.9 [3⅛"]

machine quilt in a 1.2 [½"] grid

appliqué

23.8 [9⅜"]

quilt

Outline Stitch
(reddish brown, 2-strands)

28.8 [11⅜"]

* outline quilt around each of the appliqués
* cut the lining of Bag Body A with extra seam allowance

Bag Body B

7.9 [3⅛"]   handle position   7.9 [3⅛"]

machine quilt in a 1.2 [½"] grid

appliqué

23.8 [9⅜"]

28.8 [11⅜"]

Bag Body C - make 2

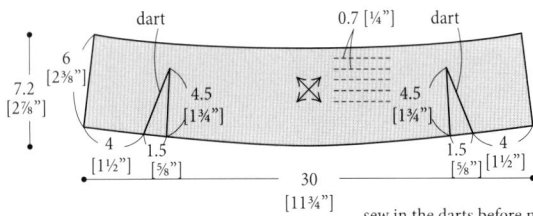

dart   0.7 [¼"]   dart

6 [2⅜"]

7.2 [2⅞"]

4.5 [1¾"]   4.5 [1¾"]

4 [1½"]   1.5 [⅝"]   1.5 [⅝"]   4 [1½"]

30 [11¾"]

sew in the darts before machine quilting

Handle

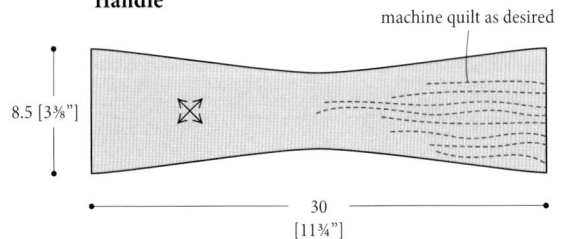

machine quilt as desired

8.5 [3⅜"]

30 [11¾"]

Bag Bottom

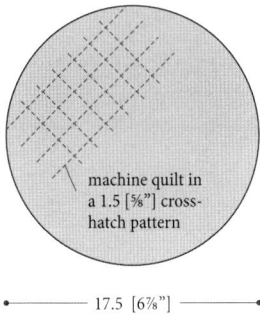

machine quilt in a 1.5 [⅝"] cross-hatch pattern

17.5 [6⅞"]

Bag Body C

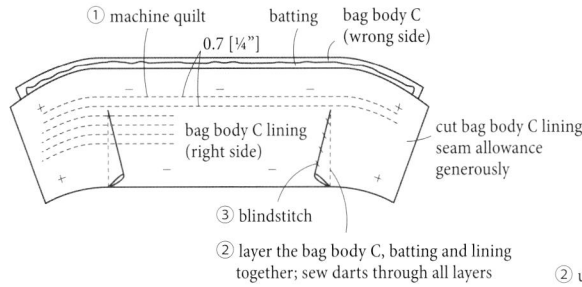

① machine quilt

batting

bag body C (wrong side)

0.7 [¼"]

bag body C lining (right side)

cut bag body C lining seam allowance generously

③ blindstitch

② layer the bag body C, batting and lining together; sew darts through all layers

with right sides together, sew bag body A and one bag body C together; repeat for bag body B and C;

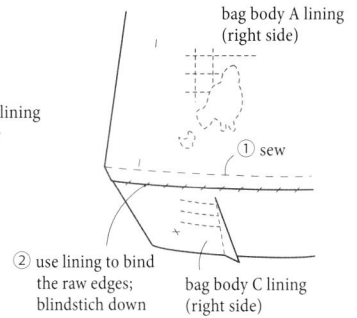

bag body A lining (right side)

① sew

② use lining to bind the raw edges; blindstich down

bag body C lining (right side)

Sewing the Bag Together

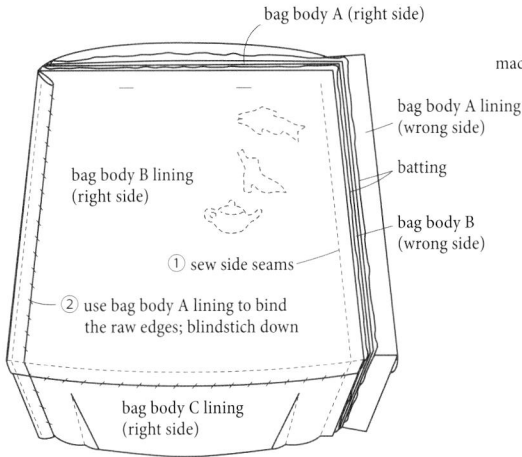

bag body A (right side)

bag body A lining (wrong side)

batting

bag body B (wrong side)

bag body B lining (right side)

① sew side seams

② use bag body A lining to bind the raw edges; blindstitch down

bag body C lining (right side)

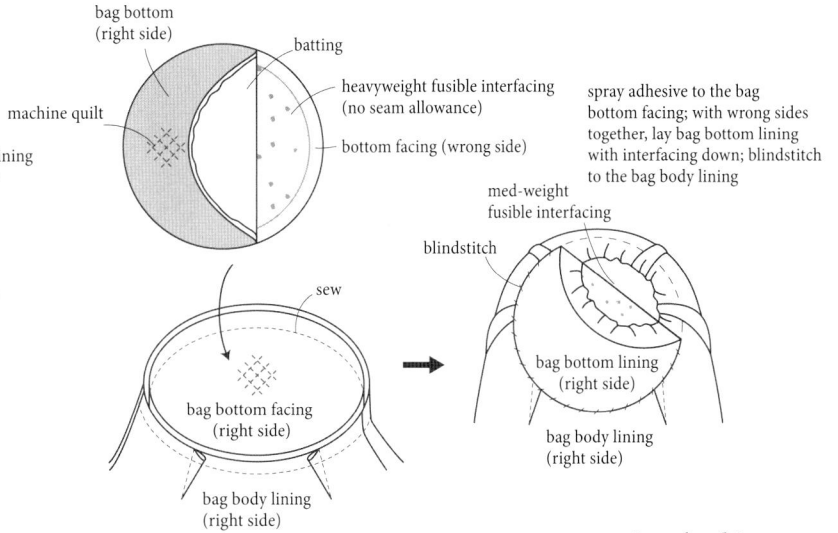

bag bottom (right side)

batting

machine quilt

heavyweight fusible interfacing (no seam allowance)

bottom facing (wrong side)

spray adhesive to the bag bottom facing; with wrong sides together, lay bag bottom lining with interfacing down; blindstitch to the bag body lining

med-weight fusible interfacing

blindstitch

bag bottom lining (right side)

bag body lining (right side)

sew

bag bottom facing (right side)

bag body lining (right side)

Making the Handle

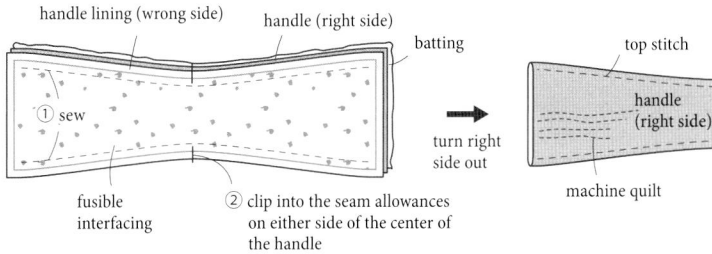

handle lining (wrong side)

handle (right side)

batting

top stitch

handle (right side)

turn right side out

machine quilt

① sew

fusible interfacing

② clip into the seam allowances on either side of the center of the handle

Completed Bag

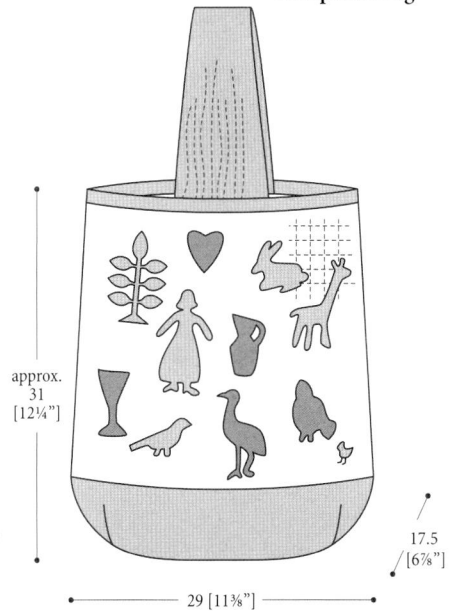

approx. 31 [12¼"]

17.5 [6⅞"]

29 [11⅜"]

Attaching the Handles

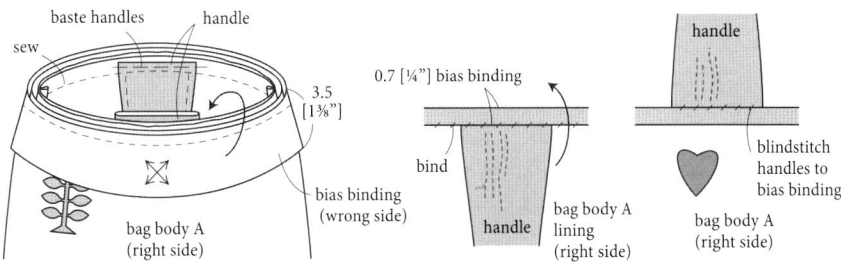

baste handles

handle

sew

3.5 [1⅜"]

bias binding (wrong side)

bag body A (right side)

0.7 [¼"] bias binding

bind

handle

bag body A lining (right side)

handle

blindstitch handles to bias binding

bag body A (right side)

PROJECTS

87

shown on p. 20

9 Around the World Shoulder Bag

The template/pattern can be found on Side B of the pattern sheet inserts.

Materials

Assorted fat quarters or scraps (piecing)
Beige stripe homespun (bag body, flap strip)
 - 80 × 40 cm [31½" × 15¾"]
Beige print (flap lining) - 40 × 30 cm [15¾" × 11¾"]
Beige print (lining, inner pocket) - 85 × 70 cm
 [33½" × 27½"]
Batting - 85 × 85 cm [33½" × 33½"]
Muslin (inner facing) - 40 × 30 cm [15¾" × 11¾"]
Grey stripe (bias binding) - 3.5 × 100 cm [1⅜" × 39⅜"]
Homespun (bias binding for seam allowances)
 - 2.5 × 70 cm [1" × 27½"]
Fusible interfacing - 80 × 40 cm [31½" × 15¾"]
Double-sided fusible interfacing - 35 × 25 cm
 [13¾" × 9¾"]
Woven webbing (strap) - 3 × 165 cm [1¼" × 65"]
2 D-rings (strap hardware) - 3 cm [1¼"]
2 Swivel clasps (strap hardware) - 3 cm [1¼"]
1 Double ring (strap hardware) - 3 cm [1¼"]
Magnetic Button - 2.2 [⅞"] 1 pair

Directions

1 Cut out the pattern pieces including the lining, facing, batting and fusible interfacing if called for.

2 Piece the design for bag flap. With wrong sides together, lay the pieced bag flap and bag flap inner facing with batting in between; baste; quilt. Fuse the double-sided interfacing to the bag flap lining and lay on the bag flap facing; baste around the sides and bottom. Sew the fabric-covered magnetic button in position.

3 Fuse the interfacing to the linings of the bag front, bag back and gusset. With wrong sides together, layer the bag front and the bag front lining with batting in between; baste; quilt. Repeat for the bag back and the gusset.

4 With right sides together, pin the bag front, bag back and gusset together; sew. Trim the seam allowances (see diagrams) and use the gusset lining to bind the raw edges.

5 Use the bias binding to bind the top edge of the bag opening; fold to the inside along the seam and blindstitch down to the lining.

6 Make the inner pocket and blindstitch the top edge to the inside of the bag back lining.

7 Pin the bag flap to the top edge of the outside of the bag back; cover with the flap strip (edges turned under to finish); top stitch to secure and cover the raw edge of the bag flap.

8 Sew the other fabric-covered magnetic button in position to the front of the bag front.

9 Sew the shoulder strap tabs with D-rings to the top edges of the gusset (see diagram). Make the shoulder strap using the woven webbing and the hardware following the diagram. Sew the shoulder strap to the hardware; Clip the shoulder straps with swivel clasps to the D-rings to finish.

Dimensional Diagram

Bag Flap

23 [9"]
0.7 [¼"] bias binding
1.2 [½"]
1.2 [½"]
32.3 [12¾"]
quilt circles 1 [⅜"] apart
24.4 [9⅝"]

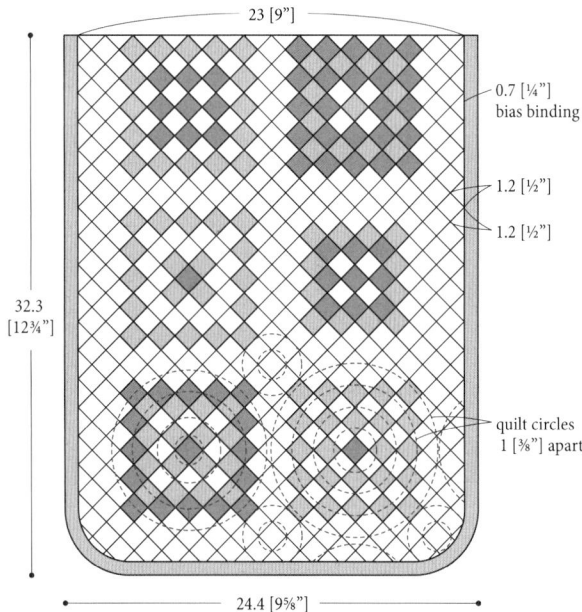

Bag Front & Back

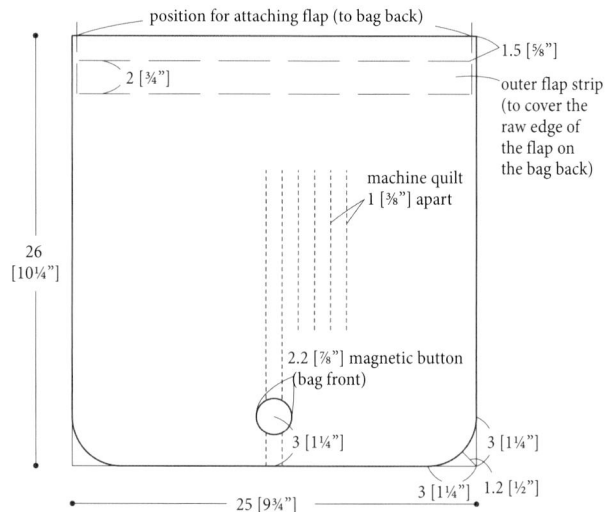

position for attaching flap (to bag back)
1.5 [⅝"]
2 [¾"]
outer flap strip (to cover the raw edge of the flap on the bag back)
machine quilt 1 [⅜"] apart
26 [10¼"]
2.2 [⅞"] magnetic button (bag front)
3 [1¼"]
3 [1¼"]
3 [1¼"]
1.2 [½"]
25 [9¾"]

Magnetic Button

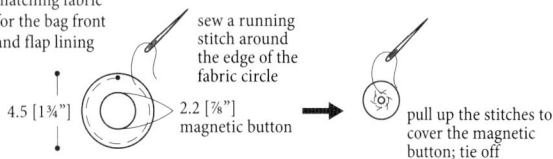

cut fabric out of matching fabric for the bag front and flap lining
sew a running stitch around the edge of the fabric circle
4.5 [1¾"]
2.2 [⅞"] magnetic button
pull up the stitches to cover the magnetic button; tie off

Gusset   cut the lining seam allowance generously

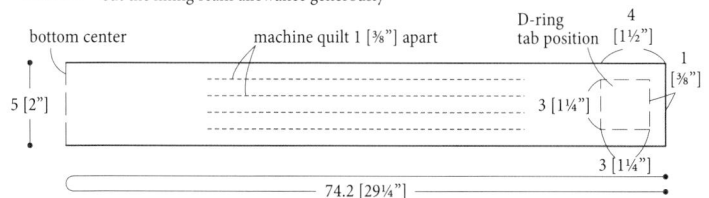

bottom center
machine quilt 1 [⅜"] apart
D-ring tab position
4 [1½"]
1 [⅜"]
5 [2"]
3 [1¼"]
3 [1¼"]
3 [1¼"]
74.2 [29¼"]

Inside Pocket

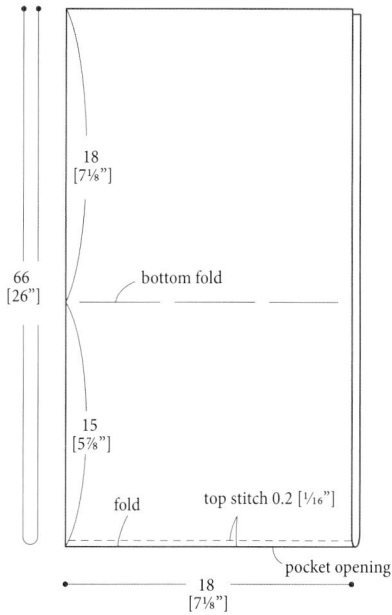

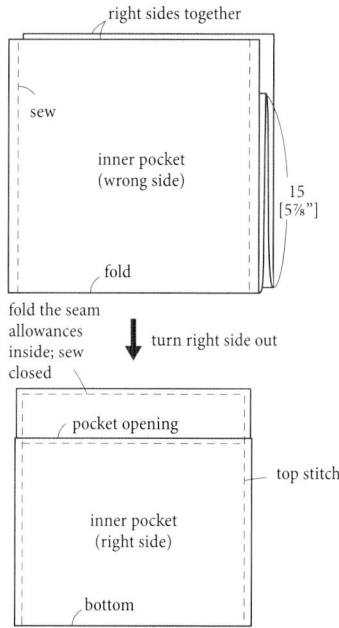

18
[7⅛"]

66
[26"]

bottom fold

15
[5⅞"]

fold

top stitch 0.2 [1/16"]

pocket opening

18
[7⅛"]

right sides together

sew

inner pocket
(wrong side)

15
[5⅞"]

fold

fold the seam
allowances
inside; sew
closed

turn right side out

pocket opening

inner pocket
(right side)

top stitch

bottom

Bag Flap

batting

flap (wrong side)

inner facing

flap lining
(right side)

double-sided
fusible interfacing

0.7 [¼"] bias binding

① sew

② sew the bias
binding around
the flap edges;
bind and blind-
stitch down to
the lining

2.2 [⅞"]
magnetic button

3.5
[1⅜"]

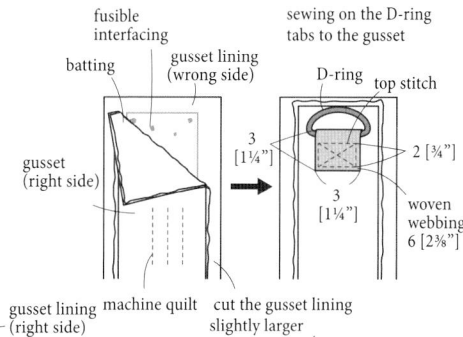

Bag Front & Back

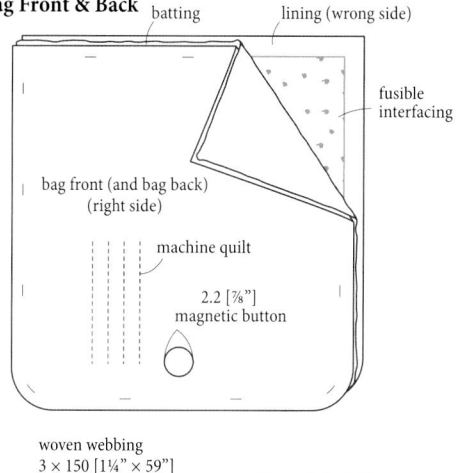

batting

lining (wrong side)

fusible
interfacing

bag front (and bag back)
(right side)

machine quilt

2.2 [⅞"]
magnetic button

woven webbing
3 × 150 [1¼" × 59"]

Completed Bag

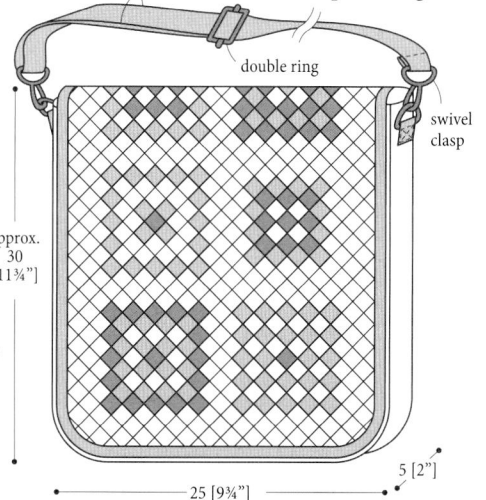

double ring

swivel
clasp

approx.
30
[11¾"]

25 [9¾"]

5 [2"]

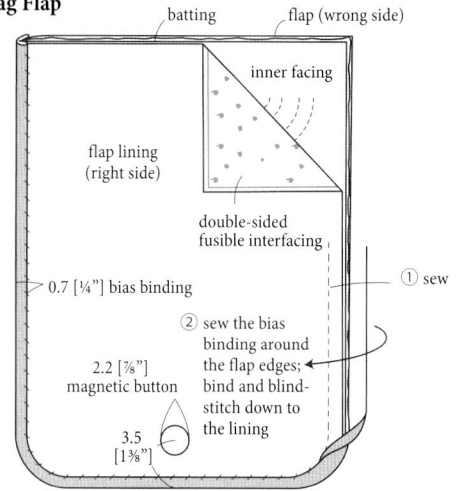

Sewing the Bag Together

with right sides together, pin the gusset and
bag front and bag back together

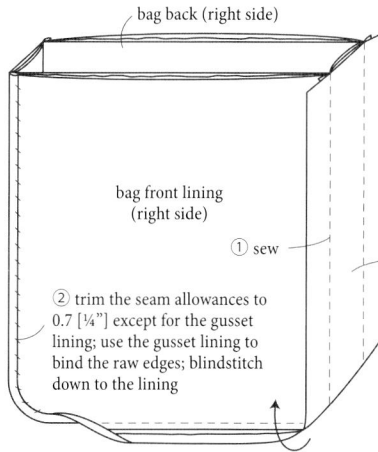

bag back (right side)

bag front lining
(right side)

① sew

② trim the seam allowances to
0.7 [¼"] except for the gusset
lining; use the gusset lining to
bind the raw edges; blindstitch
down to the lining

Gusset

fusible
interfacing

batting

gusset lining
(wrong side)

gusset
(right side)

sewing on the D-ring
tabs to the gusset

D-ring

top stitch

3
[1¼"]

2 [¾"]

3
[1¼"]

woven
webbing
6 [2⅜"]

gusset lining
(right side)

machine quilt

cut the gusset lining
slightly larger

Binding the Opening Edge

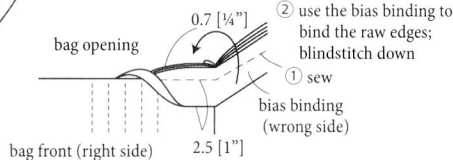

bag opening

0.7 [¼"]

② use the bias binding to
bind the raw edges;
blindstitch down

① sew

bias binding
(wrong side)

bag front (right side)

2.5 [1"]

Attaching the Flap

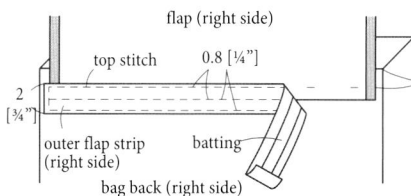

flap (right side)

top stitch

0.8 [¼"]

2
[¾"]

outer flap strip
(right side)

batting

bag back (right side)

Attaching the Inner Pocket

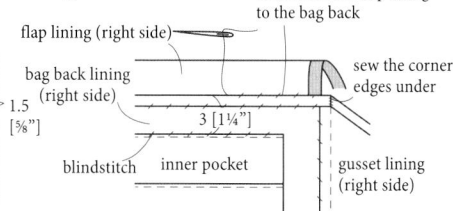

flap lining (right side)

bag back lining
(right side)

3 [1¼"]

blindstitch

inner pocket

blindstitch the flap lining
to the bag back

sew the corner
edges under

1.5
[⅝"]

gusset lining
(right side)

PROJECTS

89

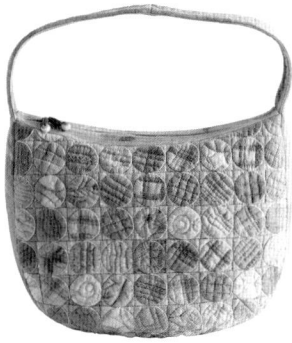

shown on p. 22 # 10 Macaroon Shoulder Bag

Materials

Assorted fat quarters or scraps (piecing and appliqué)
Grey homespun (gusset, zipper opening) - 110×30 cm
  [43¼" × 11¾"]
Homespun (lining) - 100×70 cm [39⅜" × 27½"]
Batting -100×70 cm [39⅜" × 27½"]
Fusible interfacing - 100×60 cm [39⅜" × 23⅝"]
1 Zipper - 28 cm [11"] long
Homespun (bias binding for seam allowances) -
  2.5×350 cm [1"×137¾"]
Waxed cord (zipper pull) - 30 cm [11¾"]
4 Beads (zipper pull)
Embroidery floss - white, colors to match

Directions

1 Cut out the pattern pieces including the lining, facing, batting and fusible interfacing if called for.
2 Appliqué, piece and embroider the designs for the bag front and bag back.
3 Fuse the interfacing to the wrong side of the bag back lining. With wrong sides together, layer the bag front and the bag front lining with batting in between; baste and quilt. Repeat for the bag back. Bind the bag opening edges and blindstitch down to the lining.
4 Fuse the interfacing to the wrong side of the gusset lining. With wrong sides together, layer the gusset front and the gusset lining with batting in between; baste; quilt. With right sides together, sew the short edges together to make the handle; use bias binding to bind the seam.
5 Align the bag front and bag back with the gusset using the marks as guides; baste; sew. Align the bias binding to the edges of the gusset; use the bias binding to bind the raw edges around the bag and the handle on each side; blindstitch down to the lining.
6 Fuse the interfacing to the wrong side of the zipper opening lining. With right sides together, layer the zipper opening and zipper opening lining on top of the batting. Sew around the edges, leaving an opening for turning. Turn right side out;
7 Lay the zipper opening facing with the right sides together in the center of the zipper opening; stitch along the guidelines as shown; carefully cut a slit down the center between the stitching; turn the zipper facing inside out to the zipper opening lining. Turn the edges under; blindstitch down.
8 Lay the right side of the zipper against the zipper facing, aligning centers, and blindstitch the edges down. Turn over; quilt the zipper opening piece and top stitch around the zipper.
9 Align the zipper opening to the top edges of the bag opening; use a Ladder Stitch to sew it to the bag. Make and attach the zipper pull to finish.

Dimensional Diagram

Bag Front

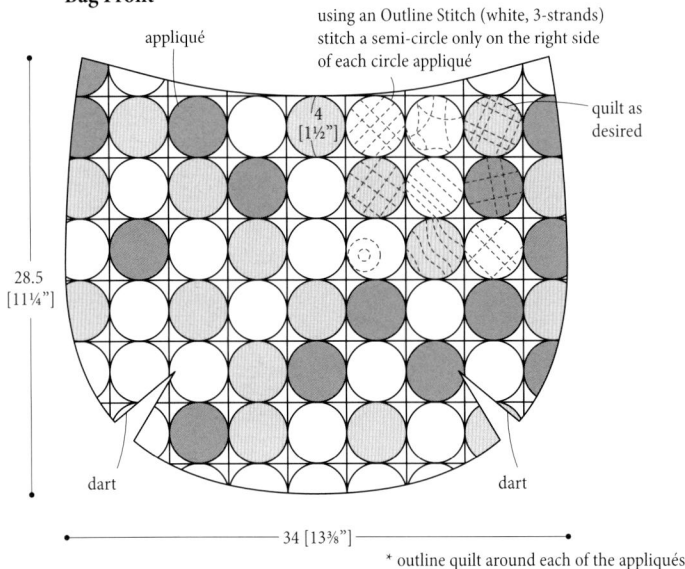

appliqué

using an Outline Stitch (white, 3-strands) stitch a semi-circle only on the right side of each circle appliqué

4 [1½"]

quilt as desired

28.5 [11¼"]

dart   dart

— 34 [13⅜"] —

* outline quilt around each of the appliqués

Bag Back

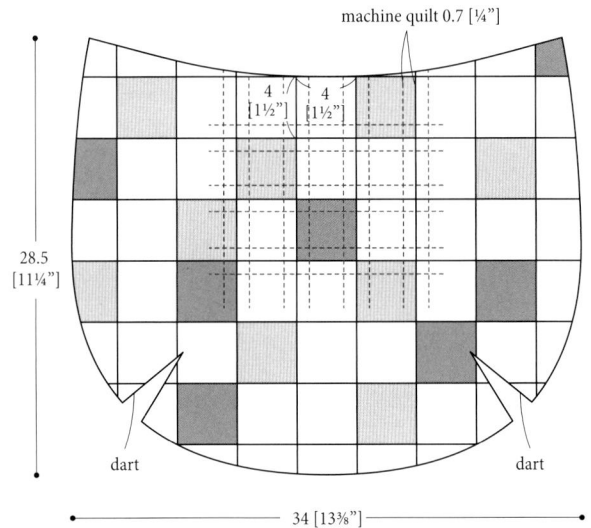

machine quilt 0.7 [¼"]

4 [1½"]   4 [1½"]

28.5 [11¼"]

dart   dart

— 34 [13⅜"] —

Gusset

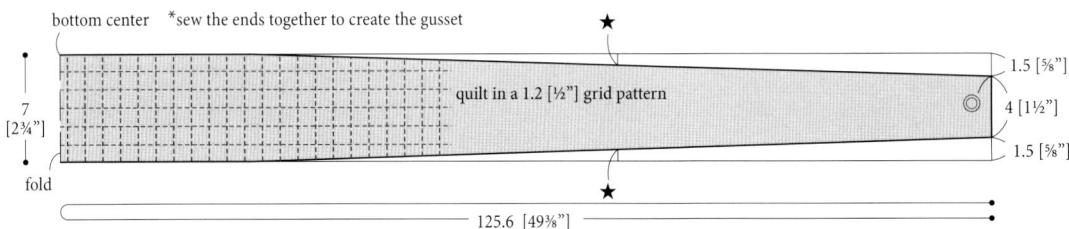

bottom center   *sew the ends together to create the gusset

★

quilt in a 1.2 [½"] grid pattern

1.5 [⅝"]
4 [1½"]
1.5 [⅝"]

7 [2¾"]

fold

★

— 125.6 [49⅜"] —

Zipper Opening

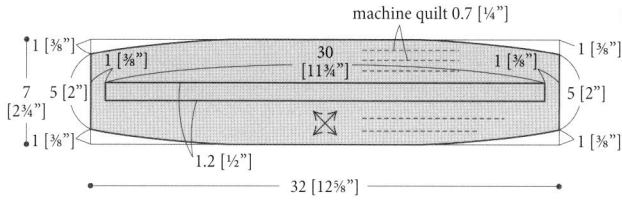

machine quilt 0.7 [¼"]
1 [⅜"]
1 [⅜"]
1 [⅜"]
1 [⅜"]
30 [11¾"]
1 [⅜"]
5 [2"]
5 [2"]
7 [2¾"]
1 [⅜"]
1 [⅜"]
1.2 [½"]
32 [12⅝"]

Making the Zipper Opening

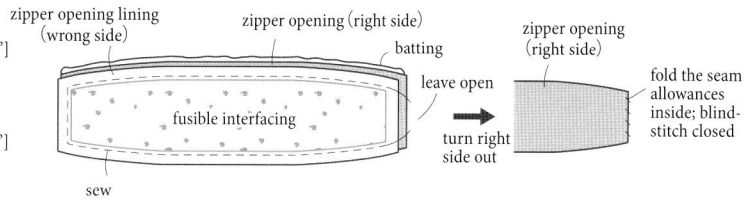

zipper opening lining (wrong side)
zipper opening (right side)
batting
fusible interfacing
leave open
turn right side out
sew
zipper opening (right side)
fold the seam allowances inside; blind-stitch closed

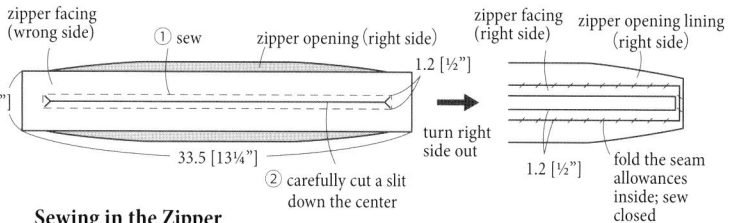

zipper facing (wrong side)
① sew
zipper opening (right side)
5 [2"]
33.5 [13¼"]
② carefully cut a slit down the center
turn right side out
1.2 [½"]
zipper facing (right side)
zipper opening lining (right side)
1.2 [½"]
fold the seam allowances inside; sew closed

Bag Body

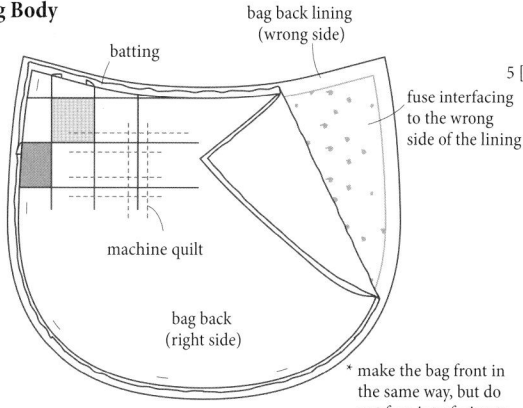

batting
bag back lining (wrong side)
fuse interfacing to the wrong side of the lining
machine quilt
bag back (right side)
* make the bag front in the same way, but do not fuse interfacing to the lining for the bag front

Sewing in the Zipper

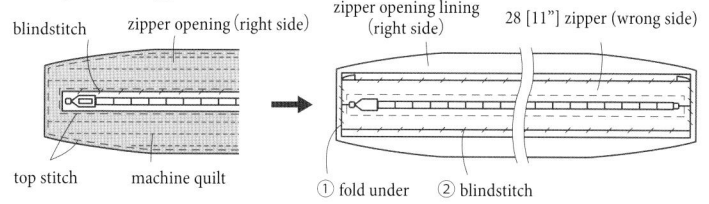

blindstitch
zipper opening (right side)
zipper opening lining (right side)
28 [11"] zipper (wrong side)
top stitch
machine quilt
① fold under
② blindstitch

Binding the Opening Edges

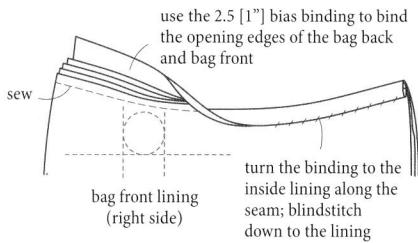

use the 2.5 [1"] bias binding to bind the opening edges of the bag back and bag front
sew
bag front lining (right side)
turn the binding to the inside lining along the seam; blindstitch down to the lining

Gusset

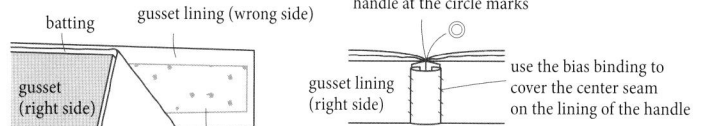

batting
gusset lining (wrong side)
gusset (right side)
fusible interfacing (no seam allowance)

sew the gusset together at the center of the handle at the circle marks
gusset lining (right side)
use the bias binding to cover the center seam on the lining of the handle

Zipper Pull

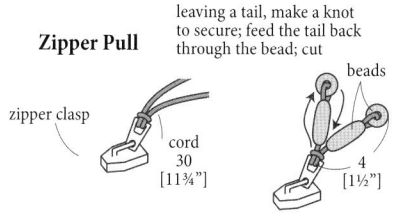

leaving a tail, make a knot to secure; feed the tail back through the bead; cut
zipper clasp
cord 30 [11¾"]
beads
4 [1½"]

Sewing the Bag Together

with right sides together, pin the gusset and bag front and bag back together

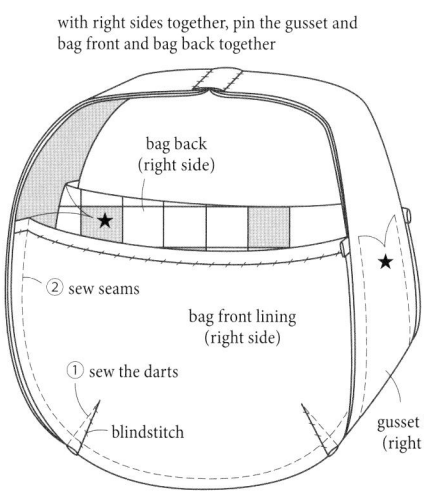

bag back (right side)
② sew seams
bag front lining (right side)
① sew the darts
blindstitch
gusset lining (right side)

Binding the Edges

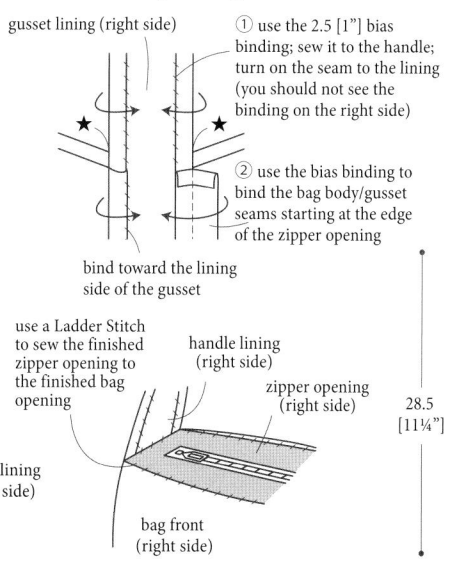

gusset lining (right side)
① use the 2.5 [1"] bias binding; sew it to the handle; turn on the seam to the lining (you should not see the binding on the right side)
② use the bias binding to bind the bag body/gusset seams starting at the edge of the zipper opening
bind toward the lining side of the gusset
use a Ladder Stitch to sew the finished zipper opening to the finished bag opening
handle lining (right side)
zipper opening (right side)
bag front (right side)

Completed Bag

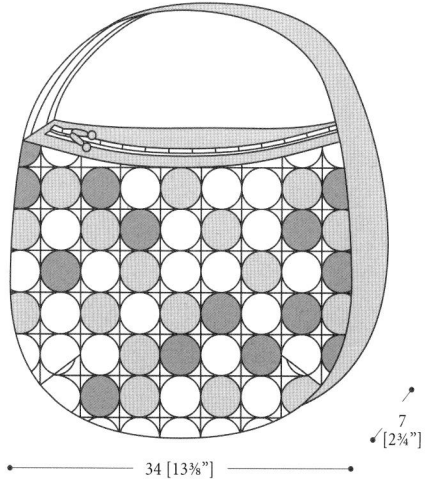

28.5 [11¼"]
34 [13⅜"]
7 [2¾"]

shown on p. 24

11 Orange Peel Handbag

The template/pattern can be found on Side C of the pattern sheet inserts.

Materials

Assorted fat quarters or scraps (bag front piecing)
Green dot print (bag front, bag back) - 110×35 cm [43¼" × 13¾"]
Print (lining) - 35×80 cm [13¾" × 31½"]
Batting - 35×80 cm [13¾" × 31½"]
Fusible interfacing - 30×35 cm [11¾" × 13¾"]
Handles (leather or faux-leather) - 1 pair

Directions

1 Cut out the pattern pieces including the lining, facing, batting and fusible interfacing if called for.
2 Piece the bag front.
3 Fuse the interfacing to the center of the wrong side of the handle lining (see diagram). With right sides together, lay the handle and handle lining against the batting. Sew along the long edges of the interfacing; trim the batting next to the stitching and turn right side out. Top stitch the handle.
4 Baste the ends of the handle to the right side of the bag front in position. Lay the lining and the batting on top of the bag front and sew across the top edge; trim the batting close to the stitching. Turn right side out; baste and quilt.
5 Fuse the interfacing to the bag back lining then repeat the steps above to make the bag back.
6 With right sides together, sew the bag front and the bag back together down the side and bottom seams. Trim the seam allowances except for the bag back lining.
7 Use the lining fabric to bind the raw edges and blindstitch down to the lining.
8 Turn the bag right side out to finish.

Dimensional Diagram

Bag Front

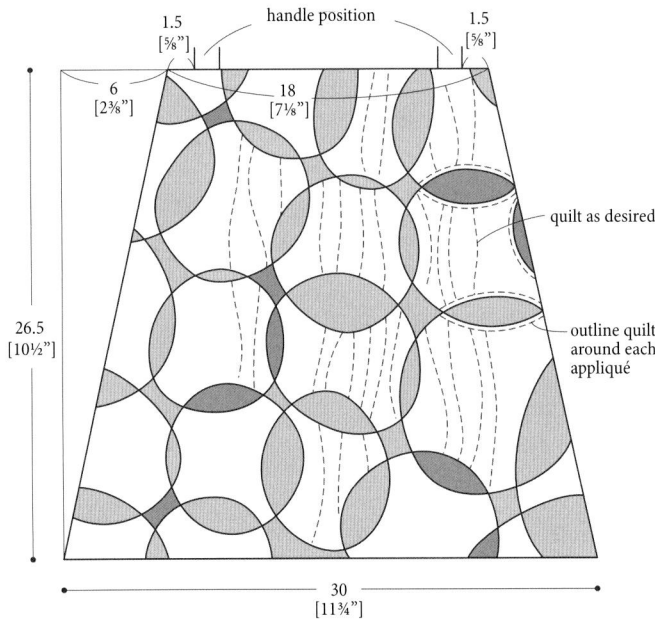

1.5 [⅝"]   handle position   1.5 [⅝"]

6 [2⅜"]   18 [7⅛"]

quilt as desired

outline quilt around each appliqué

26.5 [10½"]

30 [11¾"]

Bag Back

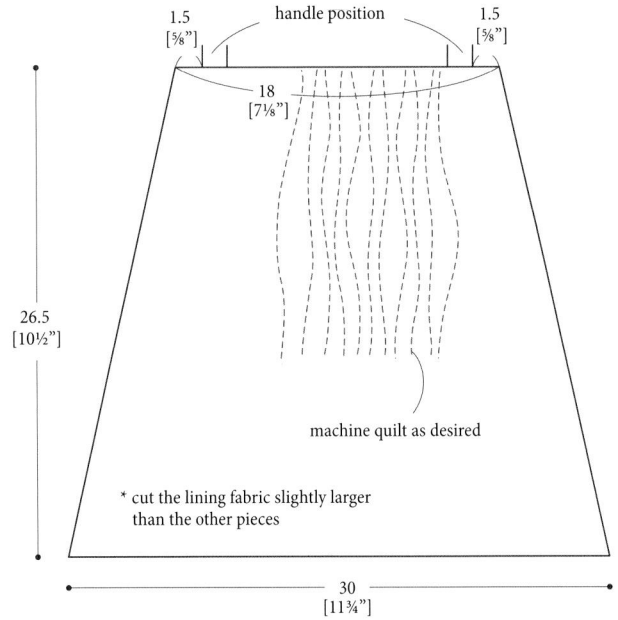

1.5 [⅝"]   handle position   1.5 [⅝"]

18 [7⅛"]

26.5 [10½"]

machine quilt as desired

* cut the lining fabric slightly larger than the other pieces

30 [11¾"]

Handles - make 2

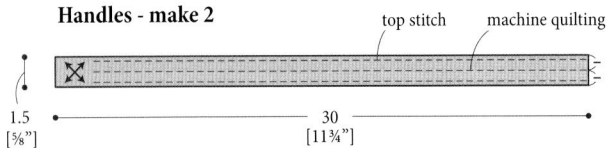

top stitch   machine quilting

1.5 [⅝"]   30 [11¾"]

Handles

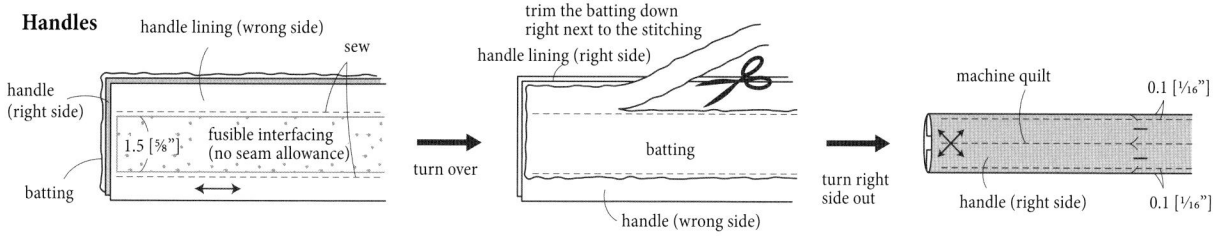

handle lining (wrong side)

sew

handle (right side)

1.5 [⅝"]

fusible interfacing (no seam allowance)

batting

turn over

trim the batting down right next to the stitching

handle lining (right side)

batting

turn right side out

handle (wrong side)

machine quilt

0.1 [1/16"]

handle (right side)

0.1 [1/16"]

Bag Front

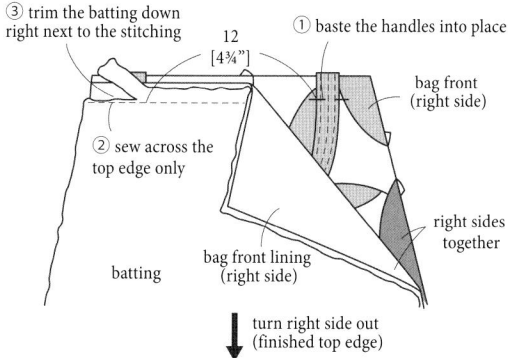

③ trim the batting down right next to the stitching

12 [4¾"]

① baste the handles into place

② sew across the top edge only

bag front (right side)

right sides together

bag front lining (right side)

batting

Bag Back

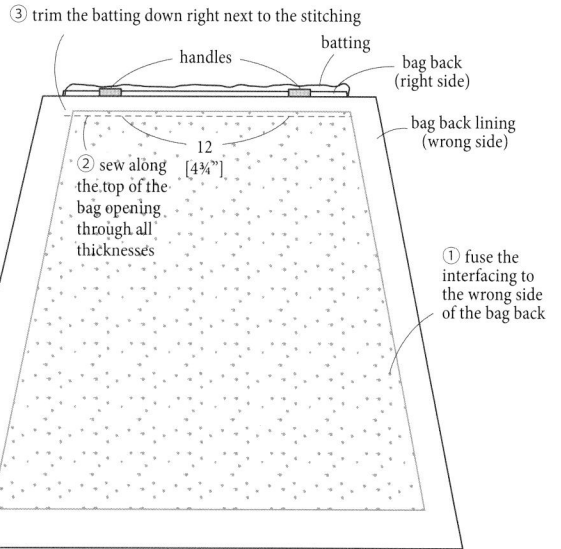

③ trim the batting down right next to the stitching

handles

batting

bag back (right side)

12 [4¾"]

② sew along the top of the bag opening through all thicknesses

bag back lining (wrong side)

① fuse the interfacing to the wrong side of the bag back

④ turn right side out with wrong sides together; pin in place; baste and quilt the bag back

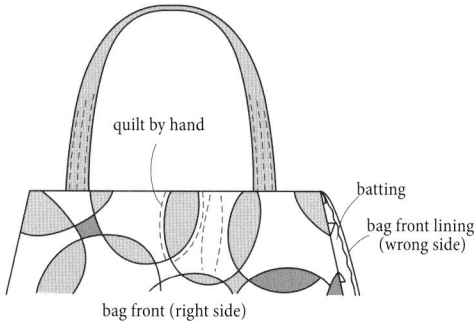

turn right side out (finished top edge)

quilt by hand

batting

bag front lining (wrong side)

bag front (right side)

Sewing the Bag Together

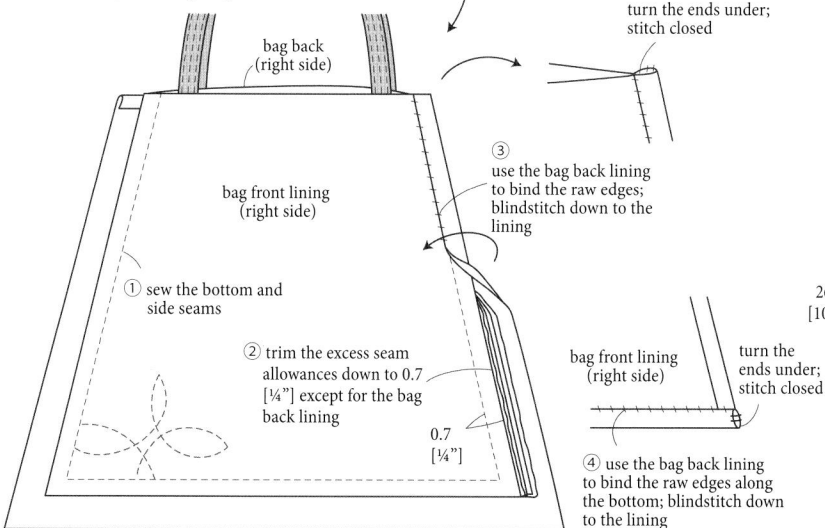

bag back (right side)

bag front lining (right side)

① sew the bottom and side seams

② trim the excess seam allowances down to 0.7 [¼"] except for the bag back lining

0.7 [¼"]

turn the ends under; stitch closed

③ use the bag back lining to bind the raw edges; blindstitch down to the lining

bag front lining (right side)

turn the ends under; stitch closed

④ use the bag back lining to bind the raw edges along the bottom; blindstitch down to the lining

Completed Bag

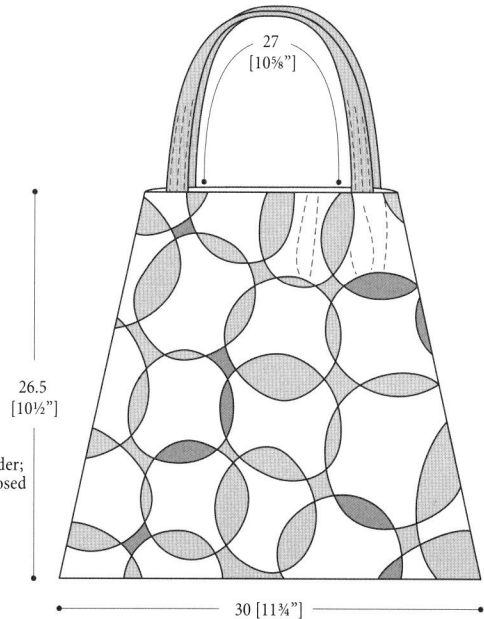

27 [10⅝"]

26.5 [10½"]

30 [11¾"]

93

shown on p. 26

12 Polka Dot Tea Time Handbag

> The template/pattern can be found on Side C of the pattern sheet inserts.

Materials

Assorted fat quarters or scraps (appliqué, handle tabs)
Dot print (bag front) - 40 × 40 cm [15¾" × 15¾"]
Black stripe homespun (bag back) - 40 × 40 cm
  [15¾" × 15¾"]
Brown stripe homespun (flap) - 30 × 50 cm [11¾" × 19¾"]
Homespun (lining) - 90 × 45 cm [35⅜" × 17¾"]
Batting - 90 × 65 cm [35⅜" × 25⅝"]
Brown plaid (bias binding) - 3.5 × 50 cm [1⅜" × 19¾"]
Homespun (bias binding for bottom gusset) - 2.5 × 30 cm
  [1" × 11¾"]
Fusible interfacing - 40 × 50 cm [15¾" × 19¾"]
Handles (leather) - 1 pair
Magnetic Button - 2 cm [¾"] 1 pair
1 Bead (zipper pull)

Directions

1 Cut out the pattern pieces including the lining, facing, batting and fusible interfacing if called for.
2 Appliqué the design to the bag front. With wrong sides together, layer the appliquéd bag front and the bag front lining with batting in between; baste and quilt.
3 Fuse the interfacing to the wrong side of the bag back lining. With wrong sides together, layer the bag back and the bag back lining with batting in between; baste and quilt.
4 With right sides together, sew the bag front and the bag back together down the side and bottom seams, leaving the corners open. Trim the seam allowances except for the bag back lining (see diagram). Bind the edges with the bag back lining.
5 Flatten the bag, aligning the side and bottom seams; sew across the raw edges to create the gusset. Trim the seam allowances and bind with a piece of bias binding.
6 Bind the bag opening with the bias binding; blindstitch down to the lining.
7 Make the handle tabs; slide through the handle hardware and sew down to the sides of the bag at the top edge.
8 Fuse the interfacing to the wrong side of the flap lining. With right sides together, lay the flap lining and the flap against the batting; sew around the edges leaving the top edge open. Turn right side out; blindstitch the opening closed. Quilt.
9 Mark the flap hole in the bottom right of the flap; cut the flap hole facing out and pin to the flap in position. Sew a 3.5 [1⅜"] circle; cut out the center of the circle and clip around the seam allowance. Turn the flap facing to the wrong side; turn under and blindstitch down.
10 Sew the magnetic button to the center of the wrong side of the flap and the center of the right side of the bag front.
11 Pin the flap to the right side of the bag back; top stitch two rows of stitching and sew the flap to the bag. Blindstitch the flap lining to the bag lining to finish.

Dimensional Diagram

Bag Front

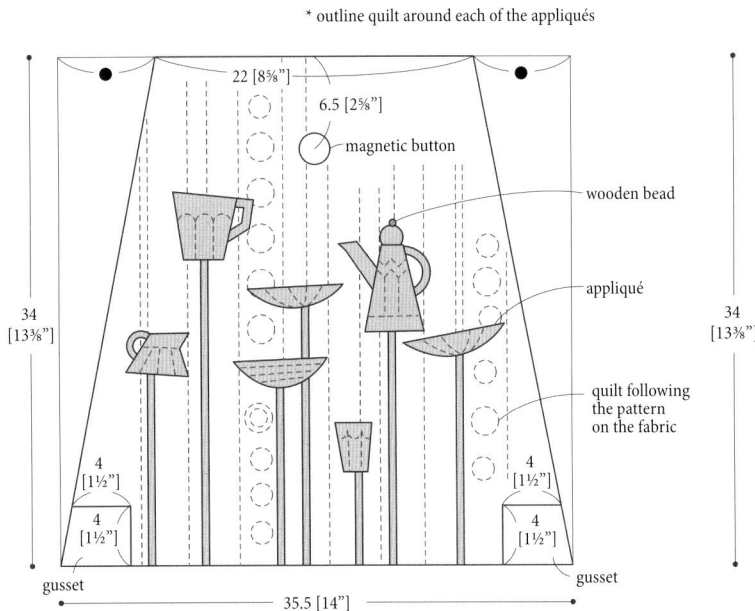

Bag Back

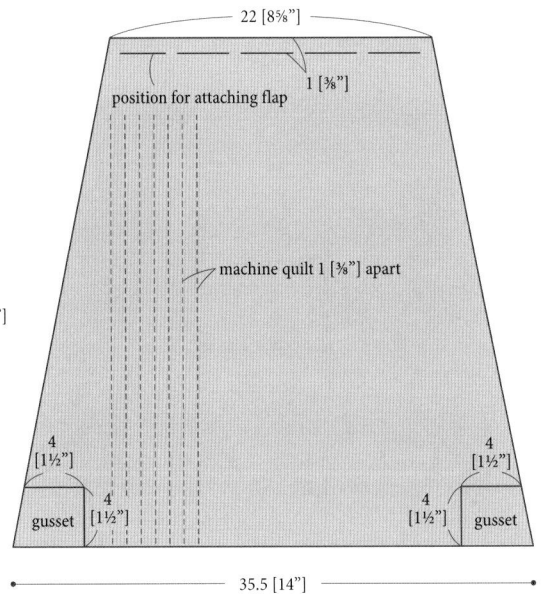

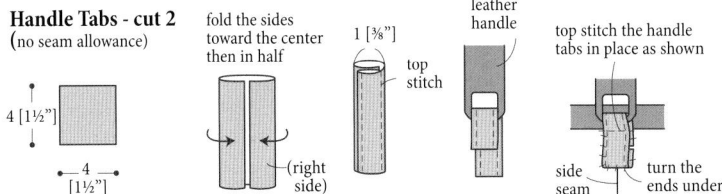

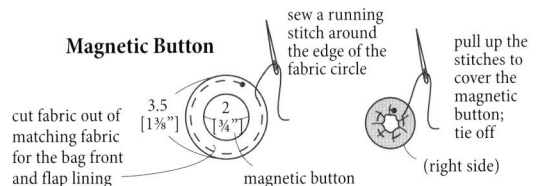

Flap

quilt following the pattern on the fabric

14.5 [5¾"]

1.5 [⅝"]

magnetic button (wrong side)

21 [8¼"]

flap lining (wrong side) flap (right side) batting

fusible interfacing

sew

turn right side out

turn the seam allowances to the inside; blindstitch the opening closed

machine quilt

flap (right side)

Making the Hole in the Flap

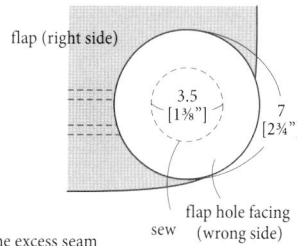

flap (right side)

3.5 [1⅜"] 7 [2¾"]

sew

flap hole facing (wrong side)

cut out the center of the circle

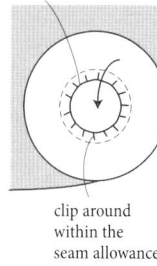

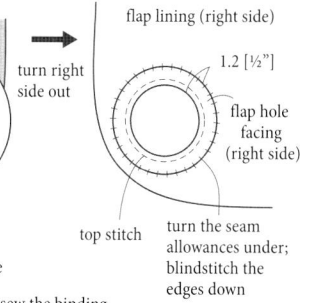

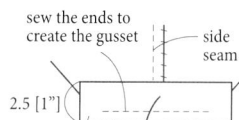

clip around within the seam allowance

turn right side out

flap lining (right side)

1.2 [½"]

flap hole facing (right side)

top stitch

turn the seam allowances under; blindstitch the edges down

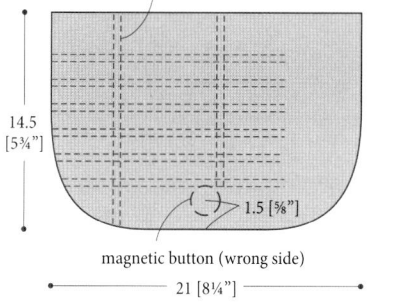

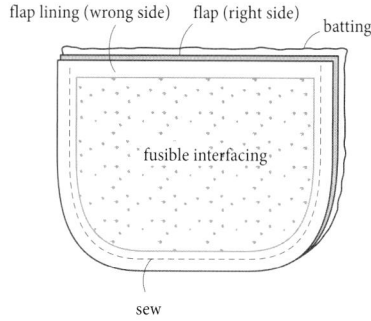

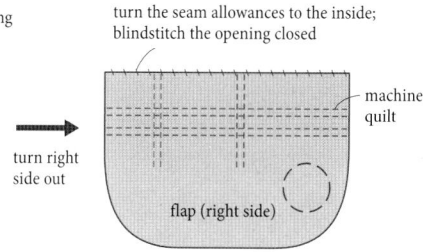

Sewing the Bag Front & Back Together

with right sides together, pin the body layers together

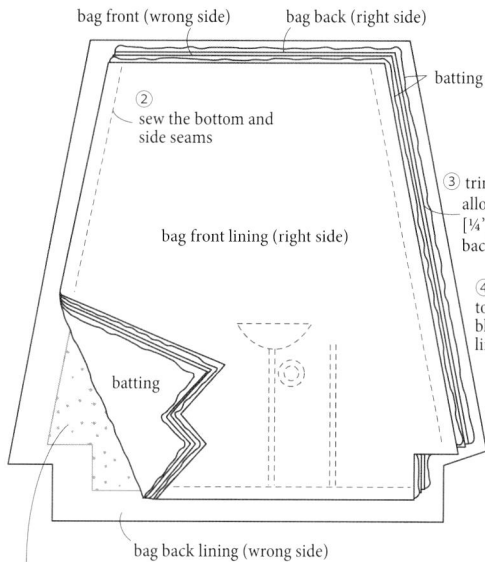

bag front (wrong side) bag back (right side)

batting

② sew the bottom and side seams

bag front lining (right side)

batting

bag back lining (wrong side)

① fuse the interfacing to the wrong side of the bag back lining (do not fuse to the bag front lining)

③ trim the excess seam allowances down to 0.7 [¼"] except for the bag back lining

④ use the bag back lining to bind the raw edges; blindstitch down to the lining

sew the ends to create the gusset

side seam

2.5 [1"]

cut a length of bias binding; lay over the flattened end; sew; trim seam allowance

sew the binding toward the bag bottom

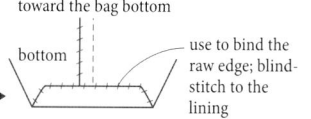

bottom

use to bind the raw edge; blind-stitch to the lining

Completed Bag

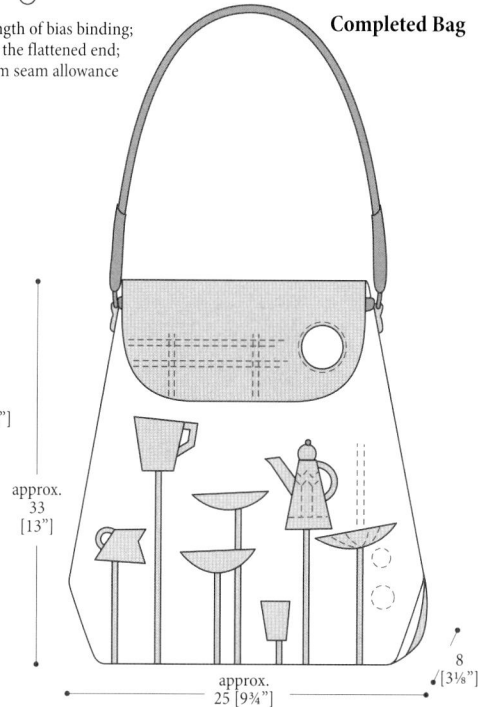

Binding the Bag Opening

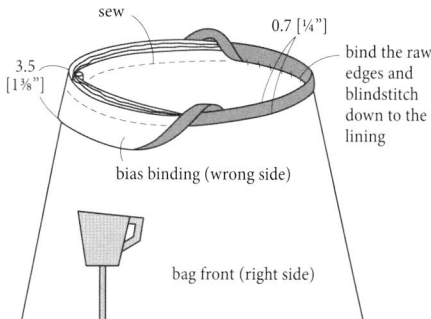

sew

0.7 [¼"]

3.5 [1⅜"]

bias binding (wrong side)

bind the raw edges and blindstitch down to the lining

bag front (right side)

Sewing on the Flap

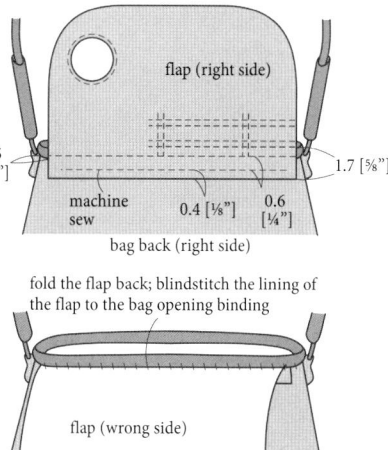

flap (right side)

0.5 [¼"]

machine sew

0.4 [⅛"] 0.6 [¼"]

1.7 [⅝"]

bag back (right side)

fold the flap back; blindstitch the lining of the flap to the bag opening binding

flap (wrong side)

approx. 33 [13"]

approx. 25 [9¾"]

8 [3⅛"]

shown on p. 28

13 Appliquéd Granny Bag

> The template/pattern can be found on Side C of the pattern sheet inserts.

Materials

Assorted fat quarters or scraps (appliqué)
Beige print (bag opening) - 25 × 35 cm [9¾" × 13¾"]
Beige stripe homespun (bag body, gusset, bag lining) -
  110 × 70 cm [43¼" × 27½"]
Beige print (bag opening lining) - 40 × 30 cm
  [15¾" × 11¾"]
Batting - 40 × 30 cm [15¾" × 11¾"]
Beige plaid (bias binding) - 3.5 × 70 cm [1⅜" × 27½"]
Woven webbing (handles) - 3 × 100 cm [1¼" × 39⅜"]
Embroidery floss - colors to match

Directions

1 Cut out the pattern pieces including the lining, facing, batting and fusible interfacing if called for.
2 Appliqué and embroider the design to the bag opening. Make two.
3 With wrong sides together, lay the bag opening and bag opening lining with batting in between; baste; quilt.
4 With right sides together, sew the bag opening pieces together along the side seams. Trim the seam allowances and use the bag opening lining to bind the raw edges (see diagram).
5 Use the bias binding to bind the top edge of the bag opening.
6 Cut the woven webbing for the handles; finish the bottom edges and pin in place on the bag opening. Top stitch them in place.
7 With right sides together, sew the two bag body pieces and gusset together. Turn right side out; stitch next to the seams, catching the seam allowance in the stitching. Pleat along the marked lines; baste in place.
8 With right sides together, and aligning edges, pin the bag opening to the bag body with the bottom edge of the bag opening at the top edge of the bag body against the pleats. Check to make sure that when you open it up, the bag body opening will be right side up; sew.
9 With the sewn bag body/bag opening piece still wrong side out, lay it on top of the bag body lining, also wrong side out. Pin the bag body and bag body lining together along one of the side seam allowances (note that you have two side seams due to the gusset; choose only one side to sew. Start to sew 4 cm [1½"] down and within the seam allowance (this is just to hold the lining in place). Turn the lining right side out over the bag body. Pull the bag body opening and handles up.
10 Fold the bag opening seam allowances under, covering the bag body lining; blindstitch down. Turn the bag right side out to finish.

Dimensional Diagram

* use an outline stitch for any area not specified
* outline quilt around each of the appliqués

Bag Opening - make 2

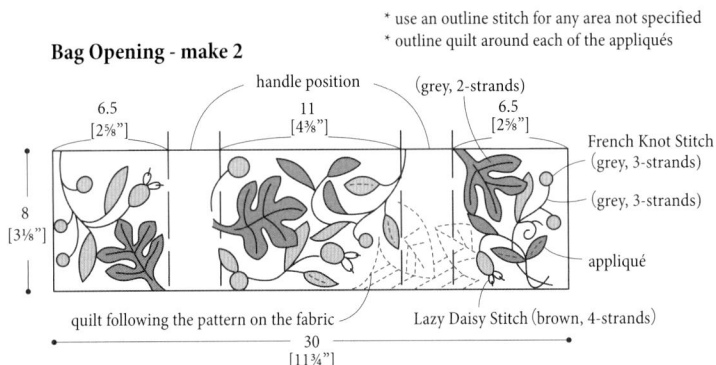

handle position

6.5 [2⅝"]   11 [4⅜"]   (grey, 2-strands)   6.5 [2⅝"]

8 [3⅛"]

French Knot Stitch (grey, 3-strands)

(grey, 3-strands)

appliqué

quilt following the pattern on the fabric

Lazy Daisy Stitch (brown, 4-strands)

30 [11¾"]

Bag Body - Bag Body Lining - cut 2 each

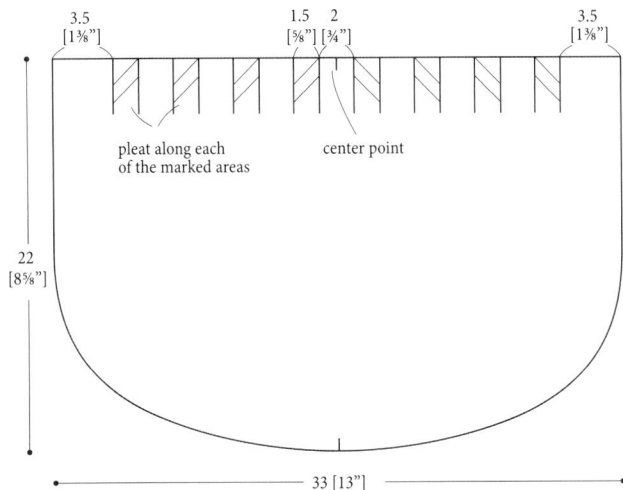

3.5 [1⅜"]   1.5 [⅝"] 2 [¾"]   3.5 [1⅜"]

pleat along each of the marked areas

center point

22 [8⅝"]

33 [13"]

Gusset - Gusset Lining

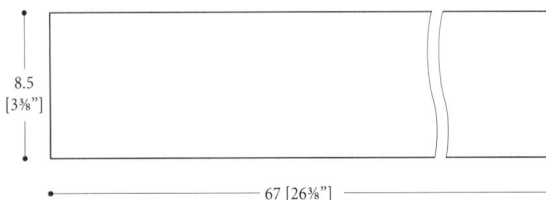

8.5 [3⅜"]

67 [26⅜"]

Bag Opening

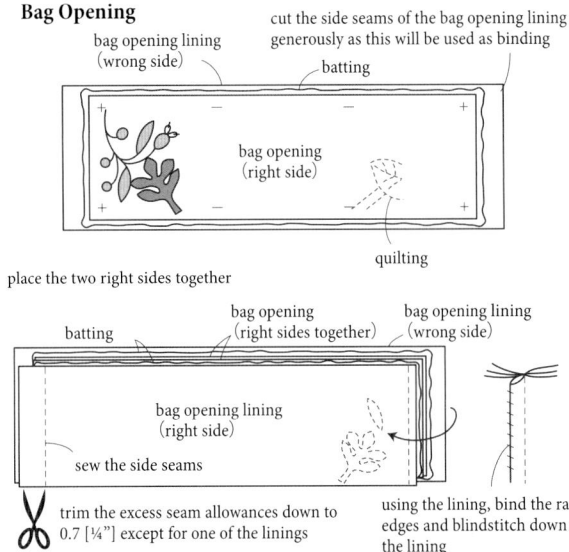

cut the side seams of the bag opening lining generously as this will be used as binding

bag opening lining (wrong side)

batting

bag opening (right side)

quilting

place the two right sides together

batting

bag opening (right sides together)

bag opening lining (wrong side)

bag opening lining (right side)

sew the side seams

trim the excess seam allowances down to 0.7 [¼"] except for one of the linings

using the lining, bind the raw edges and blindstitch down to the lining

Binding the Bag Opening Edge

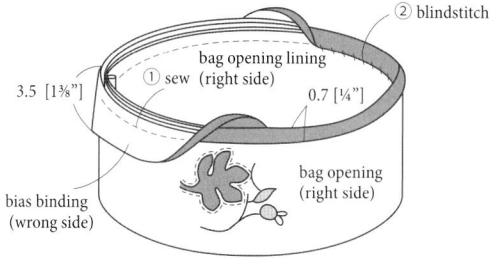

② blindstitch

3.5 [1⅜"]

① sew
bag opening lining
(right side)

0.7 [¼"]

bag opening
(right side)

bias binding
(wrong side)

Attaching the Handles

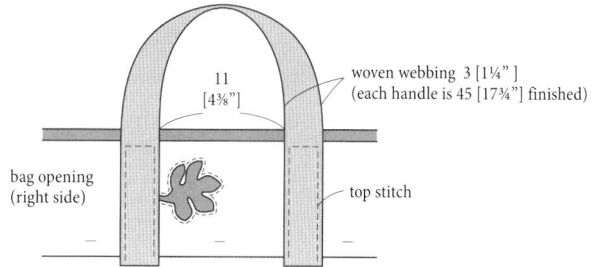

11
[4⅜"]

woven webbing 3 [1¼"]
(each handle is 45 [17¾"] finished)

bag opening
(right side)

top stitch

Sewing the Gusset to the Bag Front and Bag Back

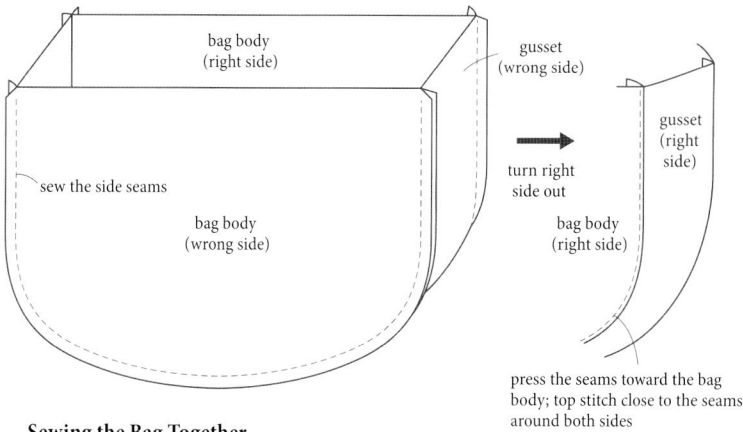

bag body
(right side)

gusset
(wrong side)

gusset
(right side)

sew the side seams

turn right
side out

bag body
(wrong side)

bag body
(right side)

press the seams toward the bag
body; top stitch close to the seams
around both sides

Sewing in the Pleats

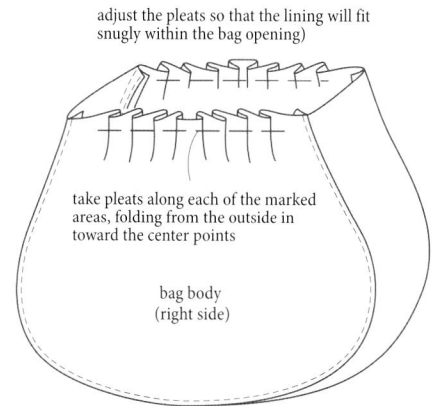

adjust the pleats so that the lining will fit
snugly within the bag opening)

take pleats along each of the marked
areas, folding from the outside in
toward the center points

bag body
(right side)

* make the bag lining in the same way as for the bag body

Sewing the Bag Together

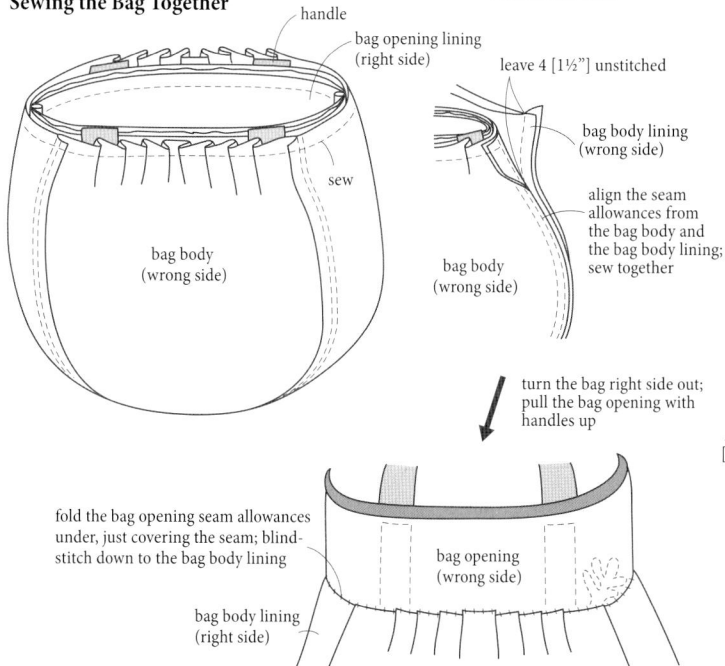

handle

bag opening lining
(right side)

leave 4 [1½"] unstitched

bag body lining
(wrong side)

sew

align the seam
allowances from
the bag body and
the bag body lining;
sew together

bag body
(wrong side)

bag body
(wrong side)

turn the bag right side out;
pull the bag opening with
handles up

fold the bag opening seam allowances
under, just covering the seam; blindstitch down to the bag body lining

bag opening
(wrong side)

bag body lining
(right side)

Completed Bag

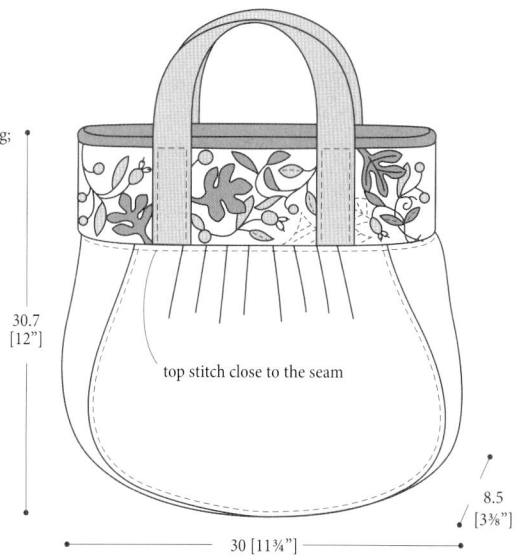

30.7
[12"]

top stitch close to the seam

8.5
[3⅜"]

30 [11¾"]

shown on p. 30

14 Modern Structural Bag

Materials

Beige print (bag body) - 90 × 20 cm [35⅜" × 7⅞"]
Brown plaid homespun (fabric strips) - 110 × 70 cm [43¼" × 27½"]
Brown homespun (bottom) - 20 × 35 cm [7⅞" × 13¾"]
Beige print (lining, handle tabs, bag bottom facing) - 110 × 45 cm [43¼" × 17¾"]
Fusible double-sided batting - 90 × 50 cm [35⅜" × 19¾"]
Batting - 40 × 25 cm [15¾" × 9¾"]
Beige check (bias binding) - 3.5 × 100 cm [1⅜" × 39⅜"]
Heavyweight fusible interfacing - 45 × 15 cm [17¾" × 5⅞"]
Double-sided fusible interfacing - 75 × 35 cm [29½" × 13¾"]
Handles (wooden) - 1 pair - 13 [5⅛"] inner diameter

Directions

1 Cut out the pattern pieces including the lining, facing, batting and fusible interfacing if called for.
2 Fuse the double-sided fusible batting between the bag body and bag body lining. Bind the top edge with the bias binding. Make two.
3 Make 38 fabric strips. With right sides together, lay the fabric strip and fabric strip lining together with fusible double-sided batting on top; sew around three sides leaving one of the short edges open for turning. Turn it right side out; press.
4 Lay 19 of the fabric strips on the right side of a bag body with the raw edges at the bottom, making sure to space them evenly. Pin them in place. Top stitch each fabric strip in place, following the diagram. Repeat for the other bag body.
5 With right sides together, lay the bag body pieces together and sew the side seams. Trim the seam allowances except for one of the bag body linings of each piece (see p. 99). Use the lining to bind the seam allowances; blindstitch down to the lining.
6 Fuse the heavyweight interfacing to the wrong side of the bag bottom facing. With wrong sides together and batting in between, baste and quilt the bag bottom. With right sides together, sew the bag bottom to the bag body.
7 Fuse the double-sided interfacing to the wrong side of the bag bottom lining. Lay the lining over the bag bottom, covering the seams and the bag bottom facing; fuse and blindstitch down to the bag body lining.
8 Make the handle tabs. Fuse the heavyweight interfacing to the wrong side of the handle tab lining. With right sides together, lay the handle tab and handle tab lining against each other. Sew around the edges leaving 6 [2⅜"] open along the top edge for turning. Turn right side out; blindstitch opening closed. Make two.
9 Backstitch the handle tabs in place at the top inner edge of the bag lining; wrap around the handle and blindstitch down to the lining to secure. Turn the bag right side out to finish.

Dimensional Diagram

Bag Body (includes bag side for both front and back) - make 2

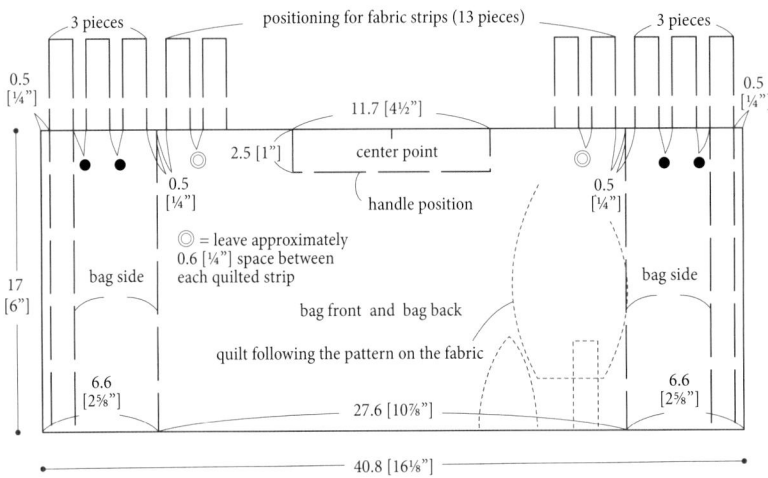

3 pieces
positioning for fabric strips (13 pieces)
3 pieces
0.5 [¼"]
0.5 [¼"]
11.7 [4½"]
2.5 [1"]
center point
handle position
0.5 [¼"]
0.5 [¼"]
◎ = leave approximately 0.6 [¼"] space between each quilted strip
bag side
bag side
17 [6"]
bag front and bag back
quilt following the pattern on the fabric
6.6 [2⅝"]
6.6 [2⅝"]
27.6 [10⅞"]
40.8 [16⅛"]

Fabric Strips - make 38

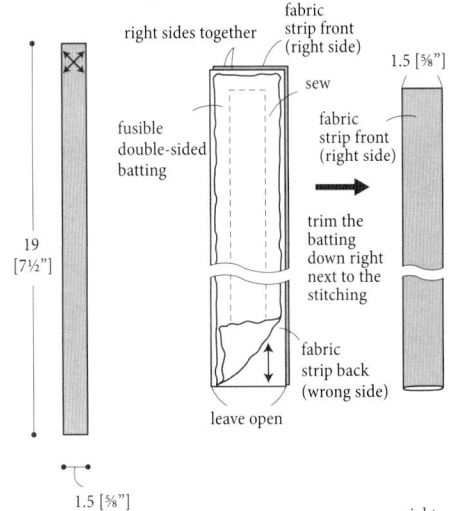

right sides together
fabric strip front (right side)
sew
1.5 [⅝"]
fusible double-sided batting
fabric strip front (right side)
trim the batting down right next to the stitching
fabric strip back (wrong side)
leave open
19 [7½"]
1.5 [⅝"]

Bag Bottom (cut the bag bottom facing the same size)

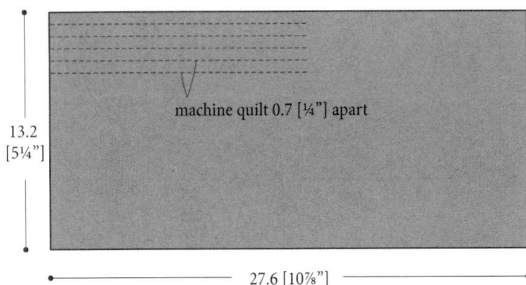

machine quilt 0.7 [¼"] apart
13.2 [5¼"]
27.6 [10⅞"]

Handle Tabs - make 2

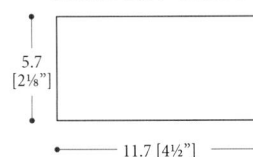

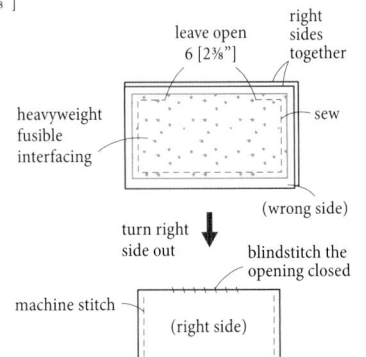

5.7 [2⅛"]
11.7 [4½"]

leave open 6 [2⅜"]
right sides together
heavyweight fusible interfacing
sew
(wrong side)
turn right side out
blindstitch the opening closed
machine stitch
(right side)

Bag Body (make 2)

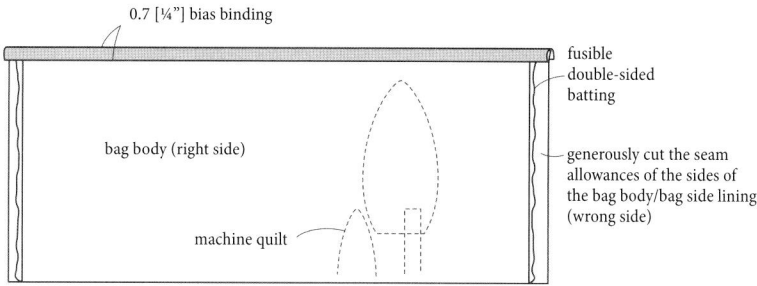

0.7 [¼"] bias binding

bag body (right side)

machine quilt

fusible double-sided batting

generously cut the seam allowances of the sides of the bag body/bag side lining (wrong side)

Sewing the Fabric Strips to the Bag Body

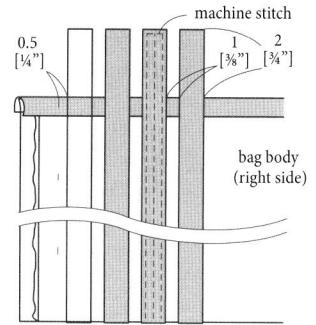

machine stitch

0.5 [¼"]

1 [⅜"]

2 [¾"]

bag body (right side)

Sewing the Two Bag Body Pieces Together
(right sides together)

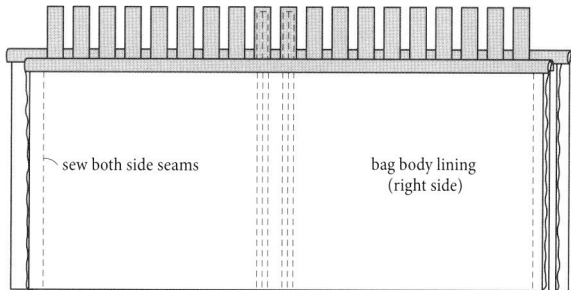

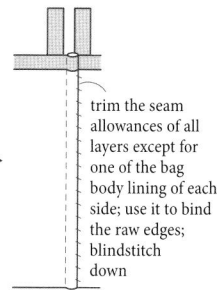

sew both side seams

bag body lining (right side)

trim the seam allowances of all layers except for one of the bag body lining of each side; use it to bind the raw edges; blindstitch down

Bag Bottom

batting

bag bottom facing (wrong side)

machine quilt

bag bottom (right side)

heavyweight fusible interfacing 13 × 27.2 [5⅛" × 10¾"]

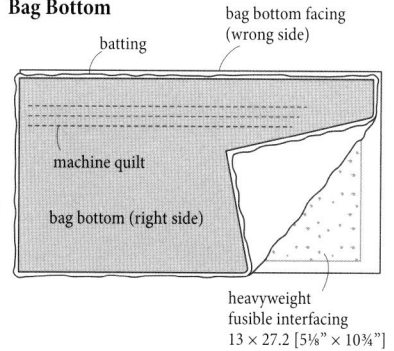

Sewing the Bag Body and Bag Bottom Together
(right sides together)

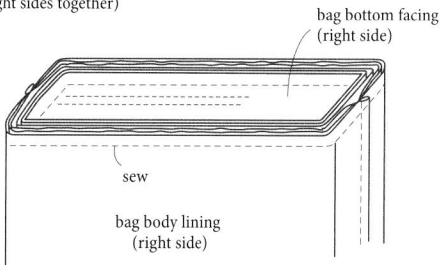

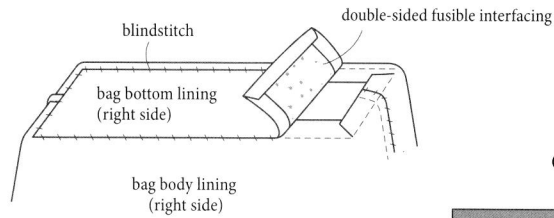

bag bottom facing (right side)

sew

bag body lining (right side)

blindstitch

double-sided fusible interfacing

bag bottom lining (right side)

bag body lining (right side)

Completed Bag

Attaching the Handles

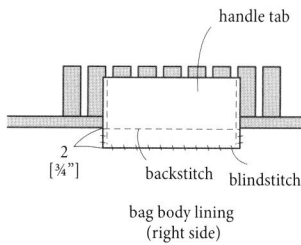

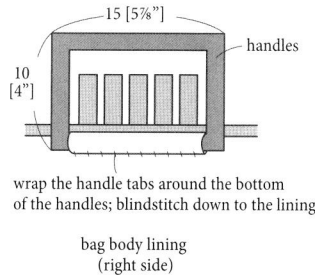

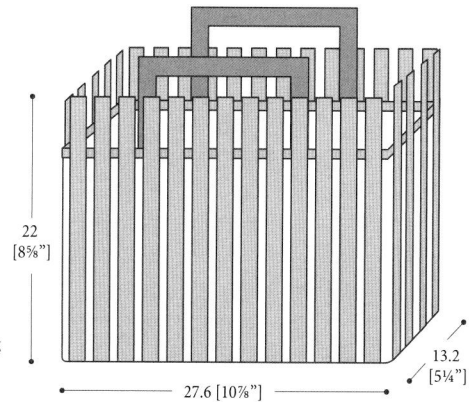

handle tab

2 [¾"]

backstitch   blindstitch

bag body lining (right side)

15 [5⅞"]

handles

10 [4"]

wrap the handle tabs around the bottom of the handles; blindstitch down to the lining

bag body lining (right side)

22 [8⅝"]

27.6 [10⅞"]

13.2 [5¼"]

shown on p. 32

15 Chic Hexagon Handbag

The template/pattern can be found on Side C of the pattern sheet inserts.

Materials

Assorted fat quarters or scraps (piecing and appliqué to make up the bag body)
Black print (lining) - 100×55 cm [39⅜" × 21⅝"]
Batting - 100×55 cm [39⅜" × 21⅝"]
Beige homespun (bias binding)
 - 2.5×300 cm [1"×118"]

Directions

1 Cut out the pattern pieces including the lining, facing, batting and fusible interfacing if called for.
2 Piece and appliqué the design to make four each of the bag body unit pieces. Make the units big enough so that after you have quilted the pieces, the pattern will easily fit with plenty of room for seam allowances (see middle diagram below).
3 With wrong sides together, lay the pieced/appliquéd bag body and bag body lining together with batting in between. Baste; quilt. Using the pattern, cut out the bag body pieces, making sure to leave a generous seam allowance for the lining as shown.
4 With right sides together, sew two of the bag body units together along one of the side seams. Trim the seam allowances except for one of the lining pieces. Use the lining to bind the raw edges; blindstitch down to the lining. Make 2.
5 With right sides together, sew the two bag body pieces together along the side seams. Use the bias binding to bind the raw edges.
6 For each of the handles, with right sides together, sew across the ends. Trim the seam allowances and use bias binding to finish the seams.
7 Using the bias binding, bind each of the bag opening and handle areas. Blindstitch down to the lining. Turn right side out to finish.

Dimensional Diagram

Bag Body (make 4 units)

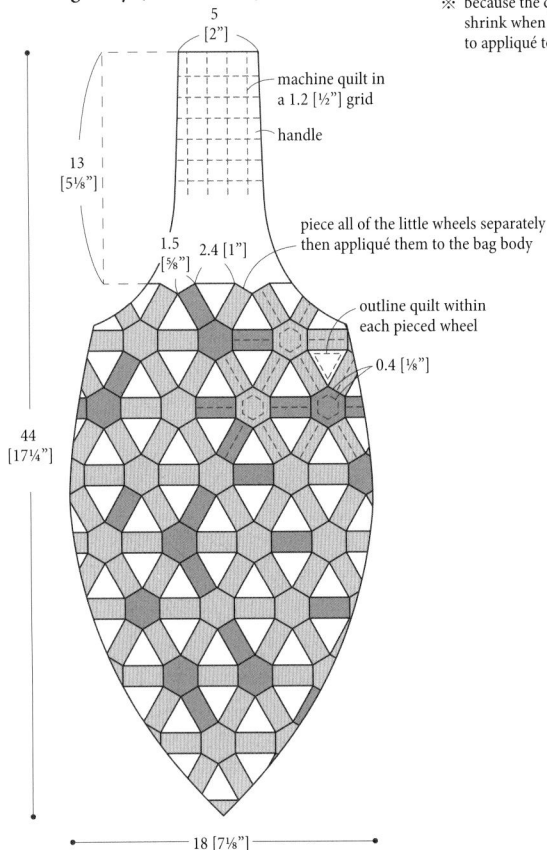

※ because the quilted bag front/bag back pieces will slightly shrink when quilting, when piecing, make plenty of wheels to appliqué to the base bag front/bag back fabric

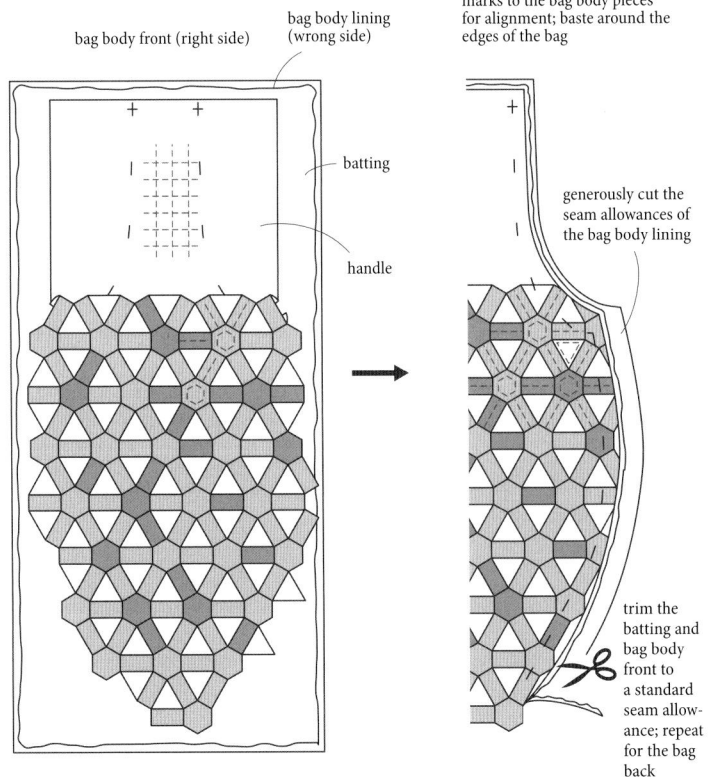

5 [2"]

machine quilt in a 1.2 [½"] grid

handle

13 [5⅛"]

1.5 [⅝"] 2.4 [1"]

piece all of the little wheels separately then appliqué them to the bag body

outline quilt within each pieced wheel

0.4 [⅛"]

44 [17¼"]

18 [7⅛"]

bag body front (right side)

bag body lining (wrong side)

batting

handle

using the pattern, transfer the marks to the bag body pieces for alignment; baste around the edges of the bag

generously cut the seam allowances of the bag body lining

trim the batting and bag body front to a standard seam allowance; repeat for the bag back

Sewing Two Bag Body Units Together to Create the Bag Body (make 2)
(right sides together)

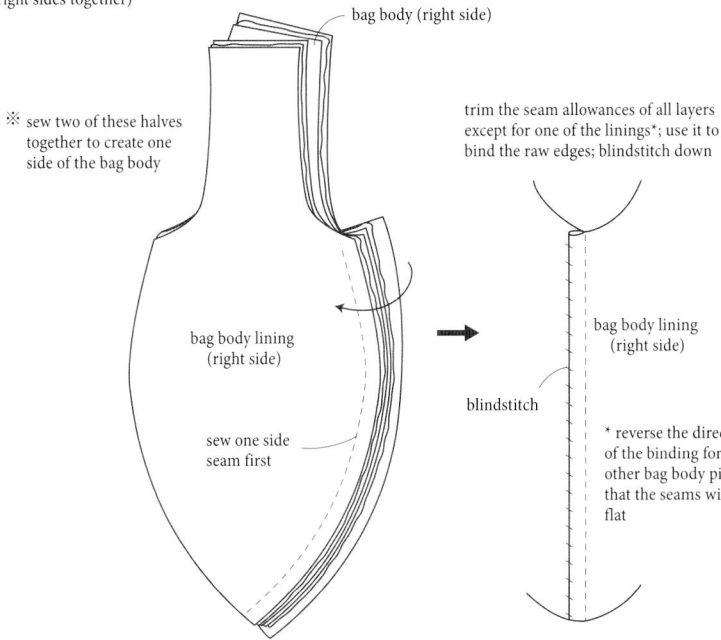

bag body (right side)

※ sew two of these halves together to create one side of the bag body

trim the seam allowances of all layers except for one of the linings*; use it to bind the raw edges; blindstitch down

bag body lining (right side)

sew one side seam first

blindstitch

bag body lining (right side)

* reverse the direction of the binding for the other bag body piece so that the seams will lay flat

Sewing the Two Bag Body Pieces Together
(right sides together)

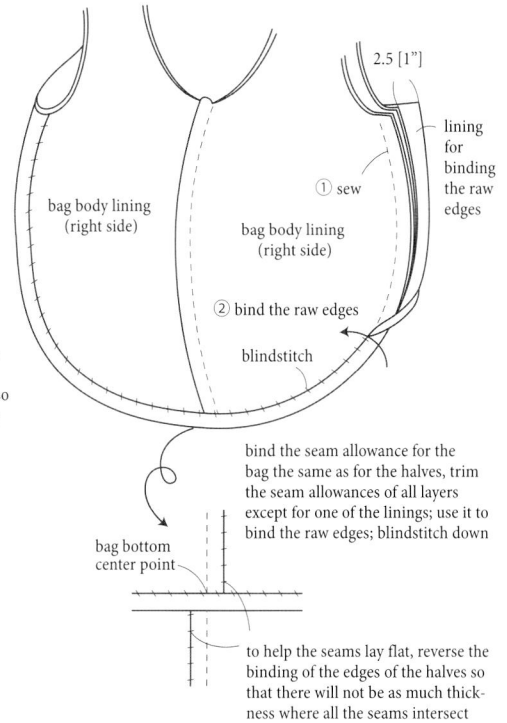

2.5 [1"]

lining for binding the raw edges

bag body lining (right side)

① sew

bag body lining (right side)

② bind the raw edges

blindstitch

bind the seam allowance for the bag the same as for the halves, trim the seam allowances of all layers except for one of the linings; use it to bind the raw edges; blindstitch down

bag bottom center point

to help the seams lay flat, reverse the binding of the edges of the halves so that there will not be as much thickness where all the seams intersect

Sewing the Handles

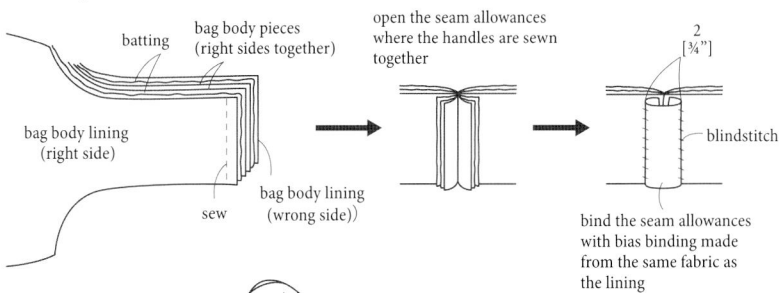

batting

bag body pieces (right sides together)

open the seam allowances where the handles are sewn together

2 [¾"]

blindstitch

bag body lining (right side)

sew

bag body lining (wrong side))

bind the seam allowances with bias binding made from the same fabric as the lining

Binding the Handles and Bag Opening

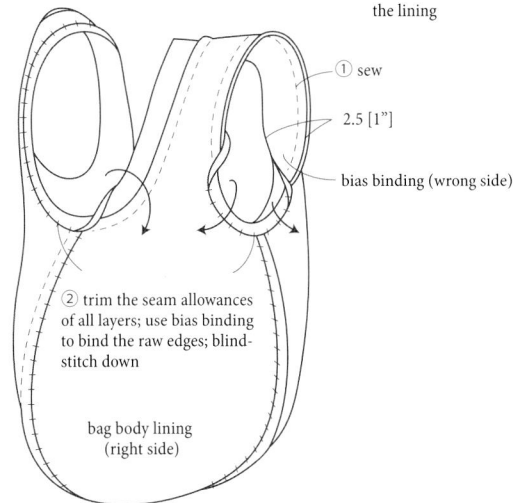

① sew

2.5 [1"]

bias binding (wrong side)

② trim the seam allowances of all layers; use bias binding to bind the raw edges; blindstitch down

bag body lining (right side)

Completed Bag

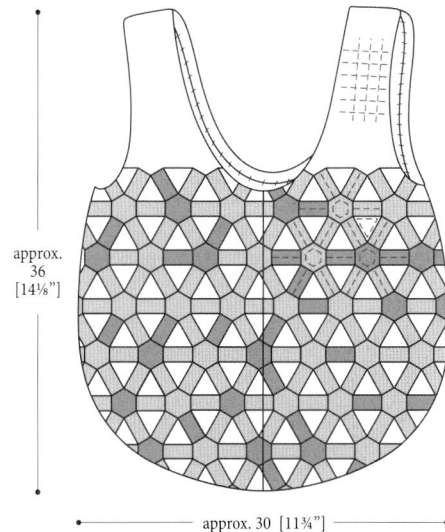

approx. 36 [14⅛"]

approx. 30 [11¾"]

shown on p. 34

16 Woolen Waist Pouch

The template/pattern can be found on Side C of the pattern sheet inserts.

Materials

Assorted fat quarters or scraps of wool (piecing and appliqué for pouch body) at least 3 of each 25 × 15 cm [9¾" × 5⅞"]

Wool (cross motif) - 15 × 15 cm [5⅞" × 5⅞"]

Navy/green stripe wool (pouch back) - 25 × 40 cm [9¾" × 15¾"]

Homespun (lining, zipper facing) - 80 × 35 cm [31½" × 13¾"]

Batting s- 80 × 30 cm [31½" × 11¾"]

Fusible interfacing - 20 × 35 cm [7⅞" × 13¾"]

1 Zipper - 23 cm [9"] long

Waxed cord (zipper pull) - 30 cm [11¾"]

3 Beads (zipper pull)

Woven webbing (belt) - 3 × 105 cm [1¼" × 41⅜"]

Buckle and slide release hardware (for belt) - 1 set

Embroidery floss - red, white or colors to match

Directions

1 Cut out the pattern pieces including the lining, facing, batting and fusible interfacing if called for.

2 Piece the pouch front. Pin the embroidered cross motif to the pouch front and appliqué in place. With wrong sides together, lay the pouch front and pouch front lining together with batting in between; baste; quilt.

3 Lay the zipper facing with the right sides together in position on top of the pouch front; stitch along the guidelines as shown; carefully cut a slit down the center between the stitching; turn the zipper facing inside out to the pouch front lining. Turn the edges under; blindstitch down.

4 Lay the right side of the zipper against the zipper facing, aligning centers, and blindstitch the edges down. Turn over; top stitch around the zipper. Sew the darts in the pouch front.

5 Fuse the interfacing to the pouch back lining. With wrong sides together, lay the pouch back and pouch back lining with batting in between; baste; quilt.

6 With right sides together and with zipper open, pin the webbing between the pouch front and pouch back; sew around the outside. Trim the seam allowances except for the pouch back lining. Use the lining to bind the seam allowances and blindstitch down to the lining.

7 Turn right side out through the zipper. Attach the buckle and slide release hardware to the webbing following the manufacturer's instructions. Finish the raw end of the belt by binding with fabric.

8 Make and attach the zipper pull to finish the pouch.

Dimensional Diagram

Pouch Front

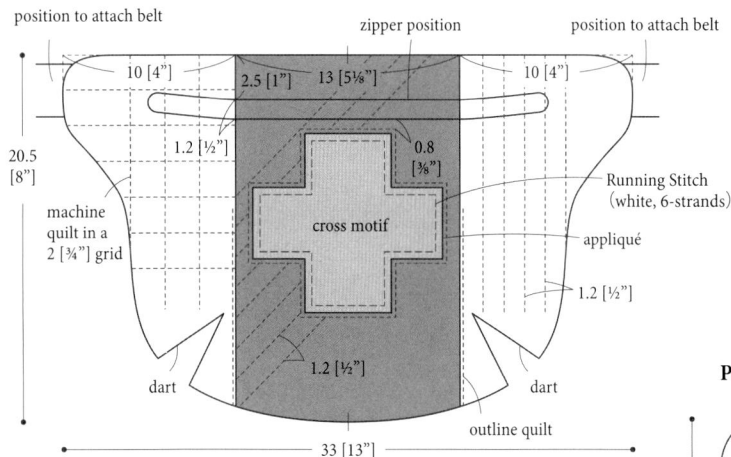

Appliquéd Cross Motif

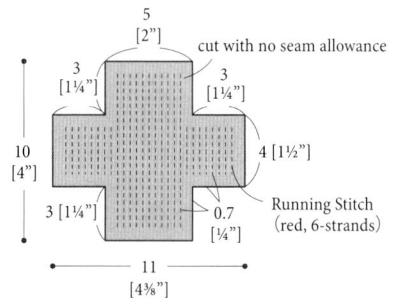

Zipper Facing

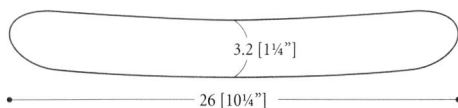

Pouch Back

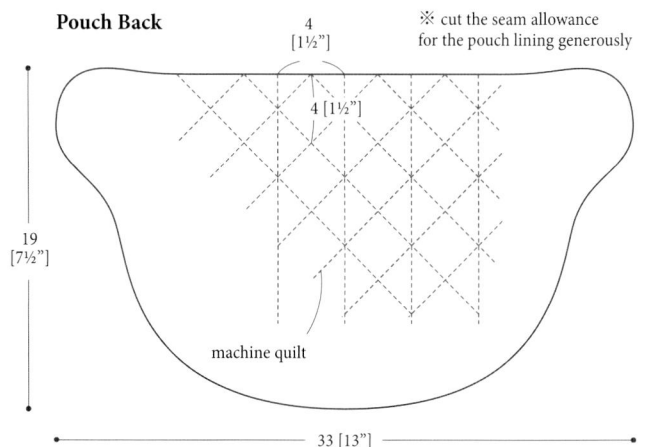

Pouch Front

pouch front lining (wrong side)

appliqué the motif on with a Running Stitch

batting

pouch front (right side)

0.5 [¼"]

machine quilt

cross motif

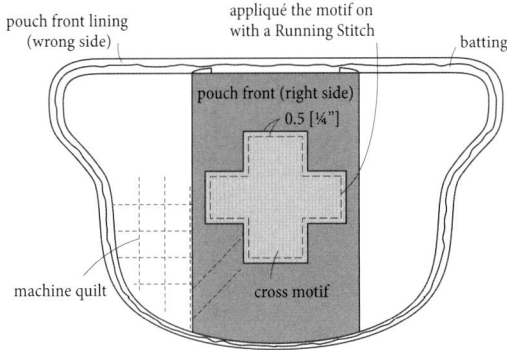

Making the Fringe

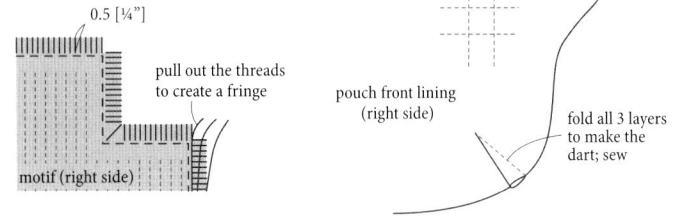

0.5 [¼"]

pull out the threads to create a fringe

motif (right side)

pouch front lining (right side)

fold all 3 layers to make the dart; sew

zipper facing (wrong side)

① sew

② carefully cut a slit down the center between stitching

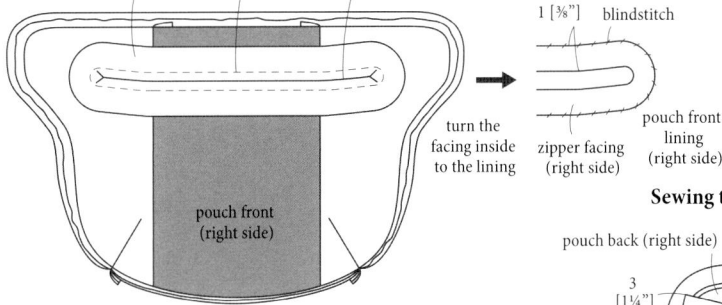

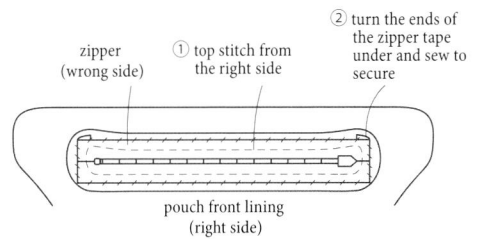

1 [⅜"] blindstitch

zipper facing (right side)

pouch front lining (right side)

turn the facing inside to the lining

zipper (wrong side)

① top stitch from the right side

② turn the ends of the zipper tape under and sew to secure

pouch front lining (right side)

pouch front (right side)

Sewing the Pouch Together

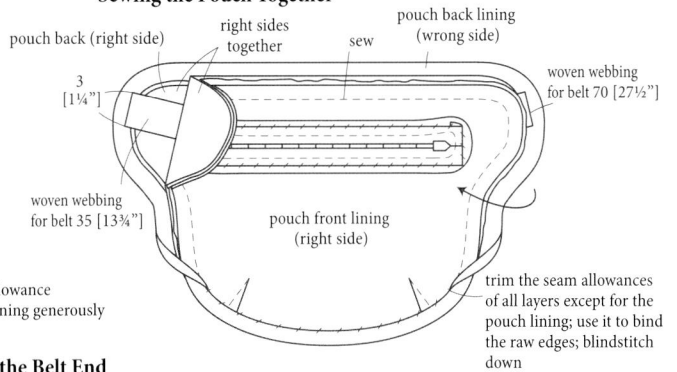

pouch back (right side)

right sides together

sew

pouch back lining (wrong side)

woven webbing for belt 70 [27½"]

3 [1¼"]

woven webbing for belt 35 [13¾"]

pouch front lining (right side)

trim the seam allowances of all layers except for the pouch lining; use it to bind the raw edges; blindstitch down

Pouch Back

batting

pouch back lining (wrong side)

fusible interfacing

cut the seam allowance for the pouch lining generously

pouch back (right side)

machine quilt

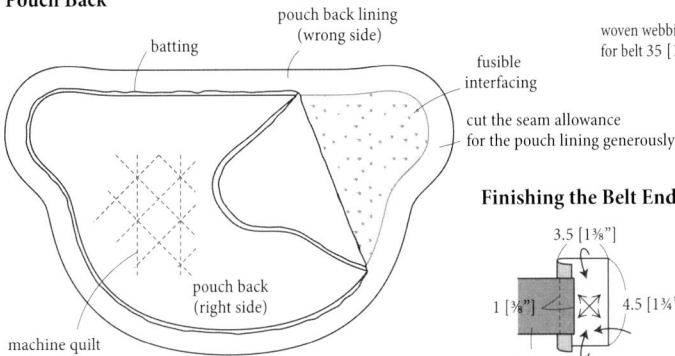

Finishing the Belt End

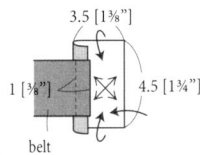

3.5 [1⅜"]

1 [⅜"]   4.5 [1¼"]

belt

Completed Pouch

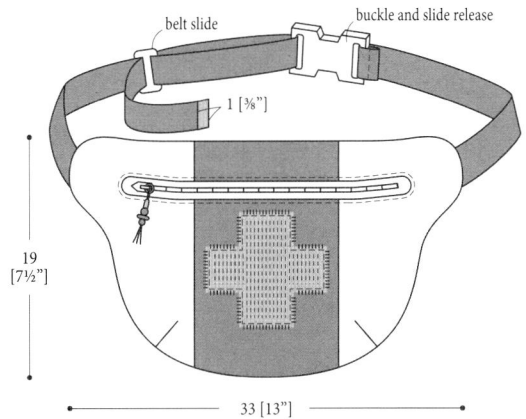

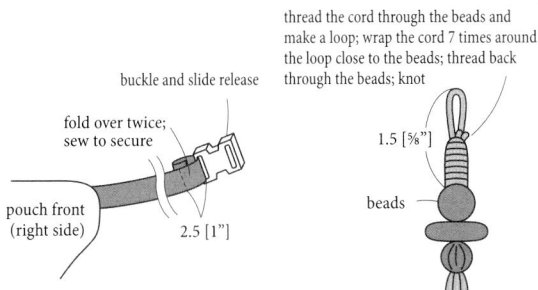

belt slide

buckle and slide release

1 [⅜"]

19 [7½"]

33 [13"]

buckle and slide release

fold over twice; sew to secure

pouch front (right side)

2.5 [1"]

thread the cord through the beads and make a loop; wrap the cord 7 times around the loop close to the beads; thread back through the beads; knot

1.5 [⅝"]

beads

Zipper Pull

zipper clasp

jump ring

5 [2"]

knot

cut

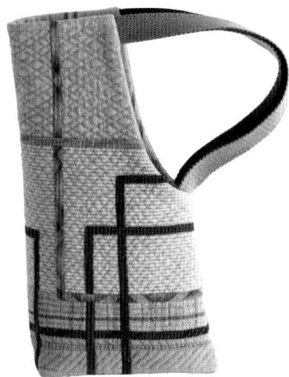

shown on p. 35

17 Contemporary Shoulder Bag

Materials

Assorted fat quarters or scraps (piecing and appliqué for bag body)

Beige homespun (lining, facing, inner pocket) - 110×90 cm [43¼" × 35⅜"]

Batting - 60×60 cm [23⅝" × 23⅝"]

Homespun (bias binding for bag bottom seam allowances) 2.5×30 cm [1"×11¾"]

Fusible interfacing - 35×50 cm [13¾" × 19¾"]

Woven cotton tape (handle) - 3×80 cm [1¼"×31½"]

1 Zipper - 16 cm [6¼"] long

Directions

1 Cut out the pattern pieces including the lining, facing, batting and fusible interfacing if called for.

2 Piece the bag body. Make bias strips for all of the appliqué lines on the bag body. Appliqué them to the bag body front.

3 With wrong sides together, lay the bag body and bag body lining together with batting in between. Baste; quilt.

4 Lay the zipper facing with the right sides together in position on top of the bag body front; stitch along the guidelines as shown; carefully cut a slit down the center between the stitching; turn the zipper facing inside to the bag body lining. Turn the edges under; blindstitch down.

4 Lay the right side of the zipper against the zipper facing, aligning centers, and blindstitch the edges down. Turn over; top stitch around the zipper.

5 Make the inner pocket (use the bag body pattern piece and measurements as a guide). With right sides together, sew along the bottom seam. Turn right side out; aligning the top and side edges, lay against the bag body lining and blindstitch the bottom and fold to the bag body lining.

6 With right sides together, sew the side and bottom seams of the bag. Trim the seam allowances except for the lining. Use the lining to bind the raw edges; blindstitch down.

7 Flatten the front corner of the bag, centering the bottom seam; sew across the tip to create the gusset. Cut off the tip and bind with a piece of bias binding.

8 Fuse the interfacing to the wrong side of the bag facing (use the bag body pattern piece as a guide). Sew the ends to create a continuous piece. Pin the handles (made of the cotton tape) in position. With right sides together, pin the bag facing to the bag body, aligning edges; sew.

9 Turn the facing to the inside; turn the seam allowances under; blindstitch down to the lining to finish.

Dimensional Diagram

Bag Body

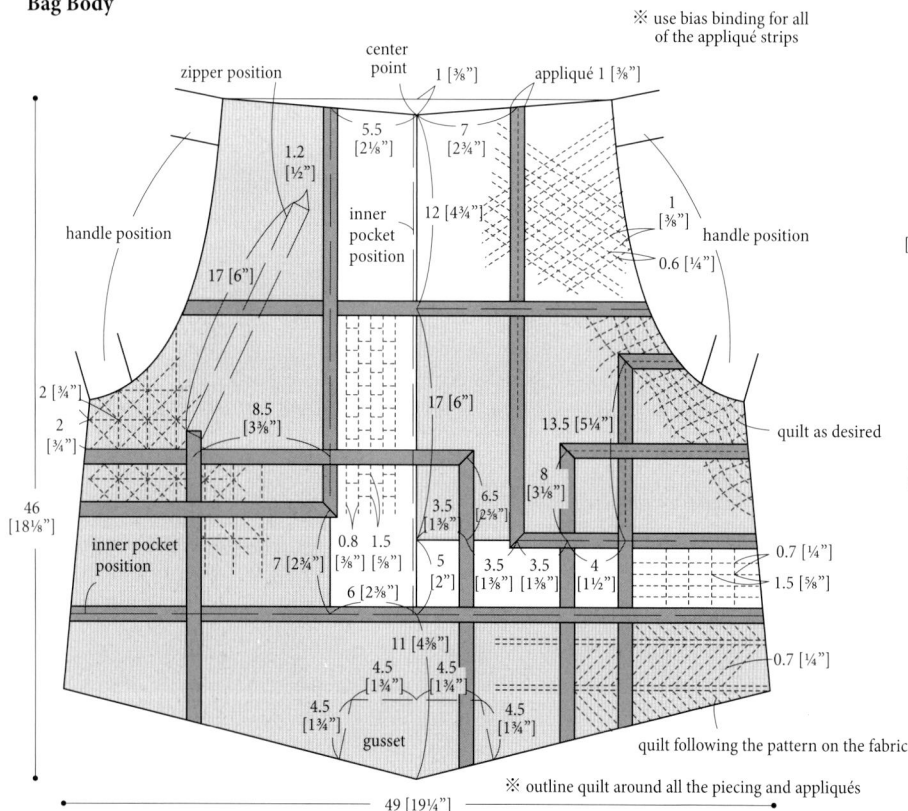

※ use bias binding for all of the appliqué strips

※ outline quilt around all the piecing and appliqués

Bag Facing

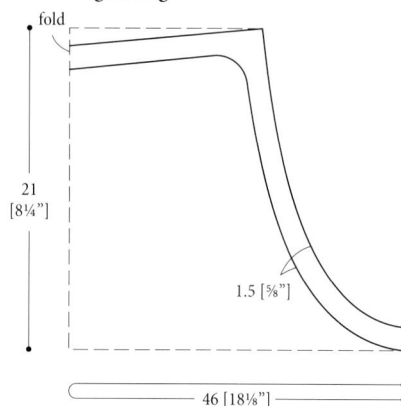

Piecing the Bag Body (right side)

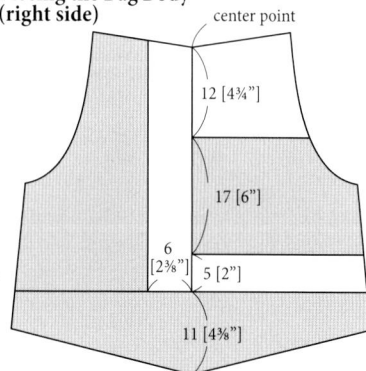

Bag Body

sew

batting

bag body lining (wrong side)

zipper facing (wrong side)

quilting

carefully cut a slit down the center between stitching

5 [2"]

21 [8¼"]

bag body (right side)

cut the seam allowance for the bag body lining generously

bag body lining (right side)

turn the facing inside to the lining

facing (right side)

blindstitch to the lining

1.2 [½"]

zipper (wrong side)

② blindstitch

① baste the zipper to the facing; top stitch from the right side

facing (right side)

16 [6¼"]

fold the ends under

(right side)

top stitch 0.2 [1/16"]

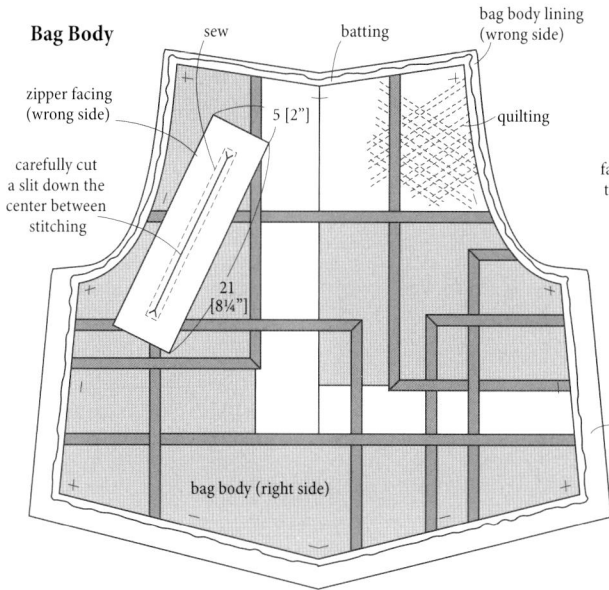

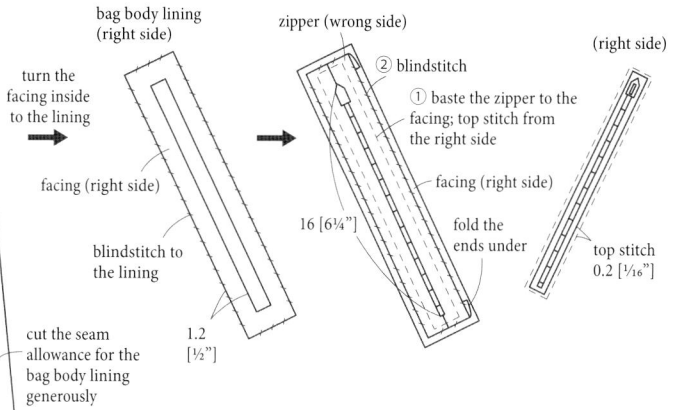

Making the Inner Pocket

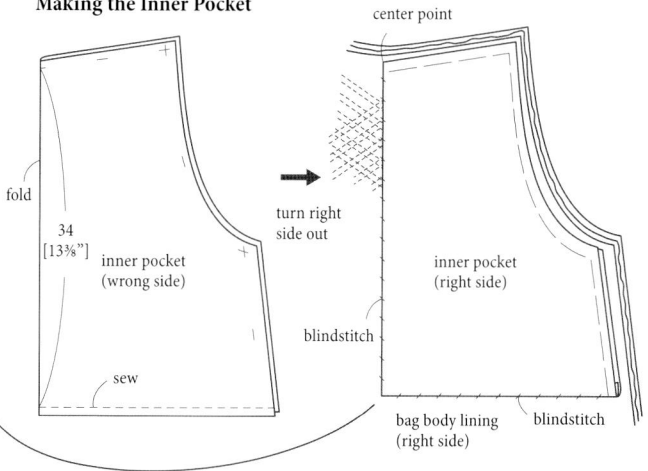

center point

fold

34 [13⅜"]

inner pocket (wrong side)

sew

turn right side out

inner pocket (right side)

blindstitch

bag body lining (right side)

blindstitch

(right sides together)

fold

bag body lining (right side)

inner pocket (right side)

sew

trim the seam allowances of all layers except for the lining on one side

Binding the Seams

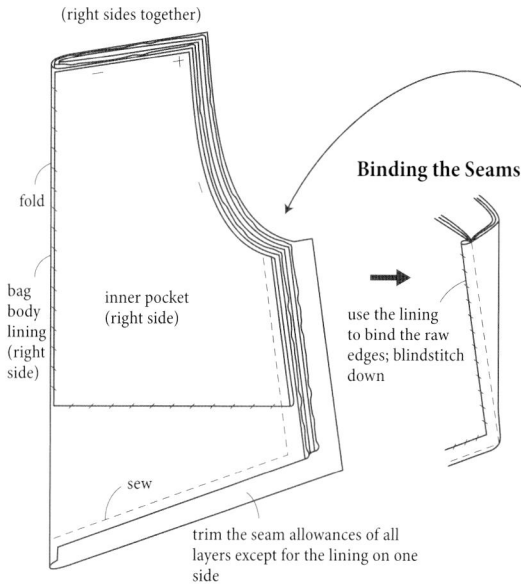

use the lining to bind the raw edges; blindstitch down

Sewing the Gusset

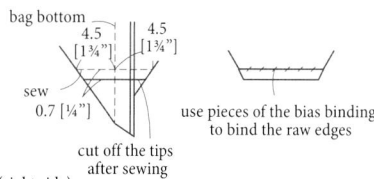

bag bottom

4.5 [1¾"]

4.5 [1¾"]

sew 0.7 [¼"]

cut off the tips after sewing

use pieces of the bias binding to bind the raw edges

Completed Bag

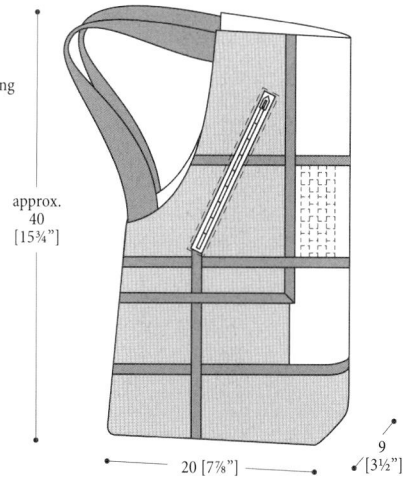

approx. 40 [15¾"]

20 [7⅞"]

9 [3½"]

Making the Bag Facing

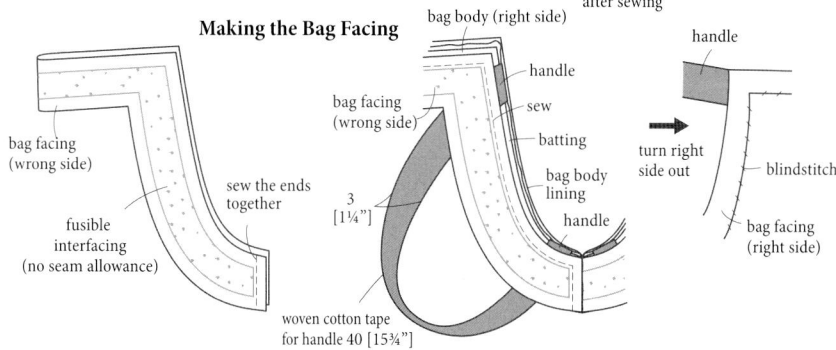

bag facing (wrong side)

sew the ends together

fusible interfacing (no seam allowance)

woven cotton tape for handle 40 [15¾"]

bag body (right side)

handle

bag facing (wrong side)

sew

batting

bag body lining

3 [1¼"]

handle

handle

turn right side out

blindstitch

bag facing (right side)

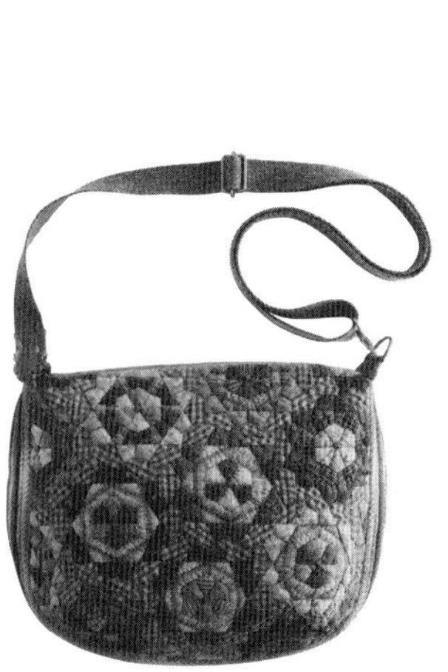

shown on p. 38

19 Patchwork Flowers Shoulder Bag

The template/pattern can be found on Side D of the pattern sheet inserts.

Materials

Assorted fat quarters or scraps (piecing and appliqué for bag front)
Brown plaid homespun (bag back, gusset, tabs, zipper pull) - 110 × 60 cm [43¼" × 23⅝"]
Grey homespun (bag back pocket) - 20 × 35 cm [7⅞" × 13¾"]
Homespun (lining) - 110 × 75 cm [43¼" × 29½"]
Double-sided fusible batting - 75 × 45 cm [29½" × 17¾"]
Batting - 40 × 80 cm [15¾" × 31½"]
Grey plaid (bias binding) - 3.5 × 35 cm [1⅜" × 13¾"]
Homespun (bias binding for seam allowances) - 2.5 × 160 cm [1" × 63"]
Fusible interfacing - 70 × 10 cm [27½" × 4"]
Magnetic Button- 2 cm [¾"] 1 pair
1 Wooden bead (zipper pull)
Woven linen tape (shoulder strap) - 2.5 × 150 cm [1" × 59"]
1 Zipper - 25 cm [9¾"] long
2 D-rings (strap hardware) - 2.5 cm [1"]
2 D-ring clasps (strap hardware) - 2.5 cm[1"]
1 Double ring (strap hardware) - 2.5 cm [1"]

Directions

1 Cut out the pattern pieces including the lining, facing, batting and fusible interfacing if called for.
2 Piece and appliqué the design to make the bag front and the gusset. Make the bag front piece big enough so that after you have quilted it, the pattern will easily fit with plenty of room for seam allowances (see diagram below).
3 With wrong sides together, lay the bag front and bag front lining together with batting in between. Baste; quilt. Repeat for the bag back. Repeat for the bag back pocket and gusset, but use double-sided fusible batting instead of regular batting.
4 Bind the top edge of the bag back pocket. Make the pocket tab with the magnetic button in it and sew it to the bag back pocket in position as shown. Lay the bag back pocket on top of the bag back aligning edges; baste.
5 With right sides together, sew the zipper to each side of the bag front and bag back; top stitch. Blindstitch the zipper tape to the lining.
6 With right sides together, pin the gusset to the bag front and bag back. Sew them together. Use the bias binding to bind the seam allowances.
7 Flatten the top of the gusset and zipper, centering the zipper; sew across the edge to create the gusset. Make the strap tabs. Sliding the D-ring through them, sandwich the gusset ends and sew them to the bag.
8 Make the shoulder strap using the woven linen tape and the hardware following the diagram. Sew the shoulder strap to the hardware; clip the shoulder straps to the D-rings to finish.

Dimensional Diagram

Bag Front

* outline quilt around the piecings and appliqués

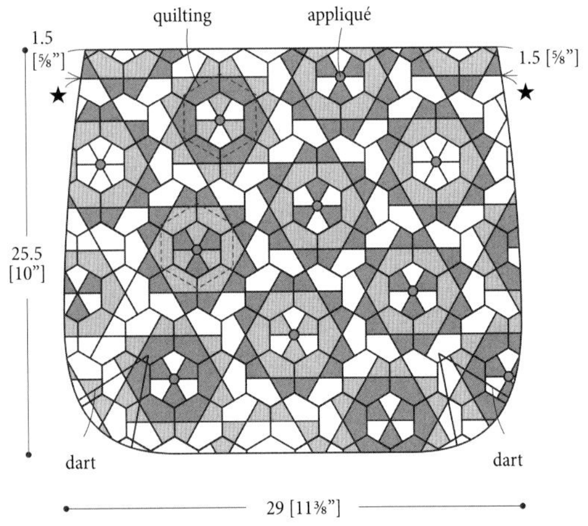
quilting
appliqué
1.5 [5/8"]
1.5 [5/8"]
25.5 [10"]
dart
dart
29 [11⅜"]

※ because the quilted bag front will shrink slightly when quilting, make sure to make plenty of the pieced/ appliquéd base fabric pieces so that the pattern will fit

Bag Back

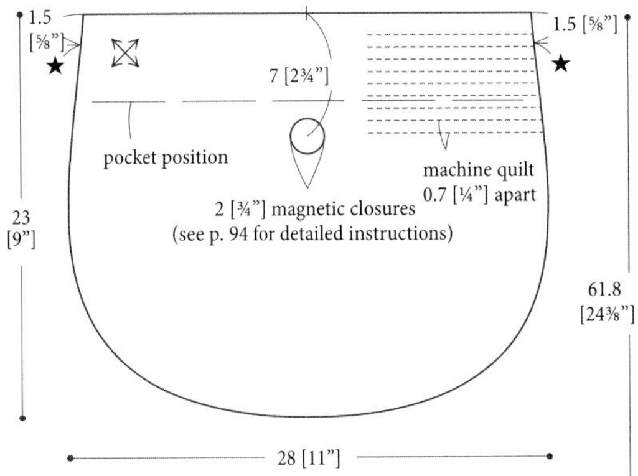
1.5 [5/8"]
1.5 [5/8"]
7 [2¾"]
pocket position
machine quilt 0.7 [¼"] apart
2 [¾"] magnetic closures (see p. 94 for detailed instructions)
23 [9"]
28 [11"]

Gusset

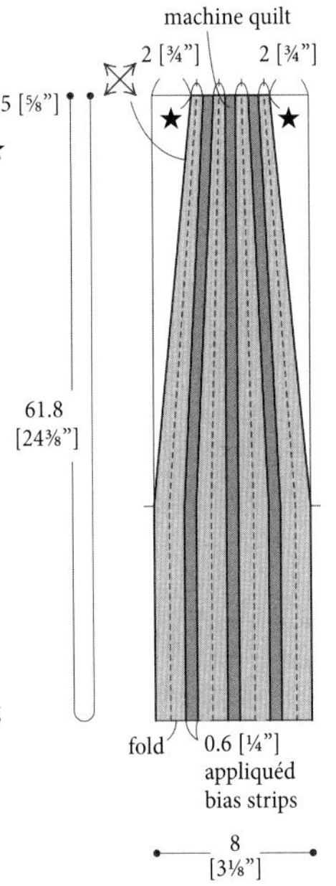
machine quilt
2 [¾"]
2 [¾"]
61.8 [24⅜"]
fold
0.6 [¼"] appliquéd bias strips
8 [3⅛"]

Bag Back Pocket

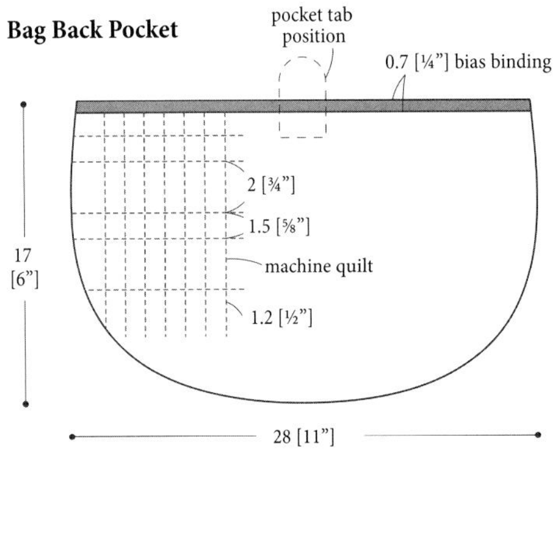
pocket tab position
0.7 [¼"] bias binding
2 [¾"]
1.5 [5/8"]
machine quilt
1.2 [½"]
17 [6"]
28 [11"]

Pocket Tab

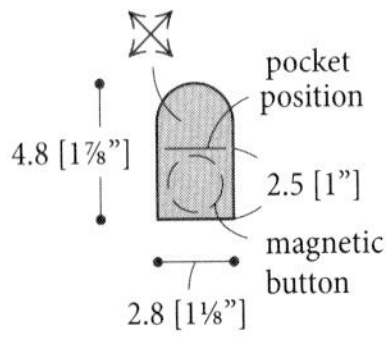
pocket position
4.8 [1⅞"]
2.5 [1"]
magnetic button
2.8 [1⅛"]

Strap Tabs (make 2)

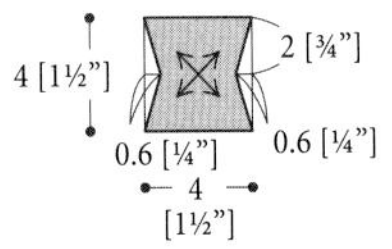
2 [¾"]
4 [1½"]
0.6 [¼"]
0.6 [¼"]
4 [1½"]

Zipper Pull

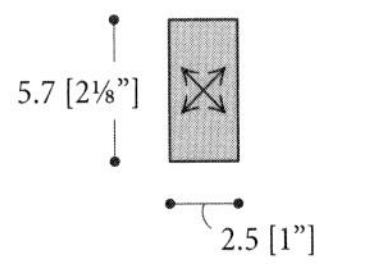
5.7 [2⅛"]
2.5 [1"]

(cut with no seam allowance)

Bag Back Pocket

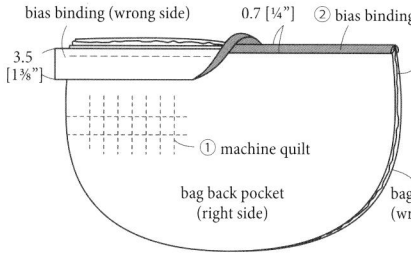

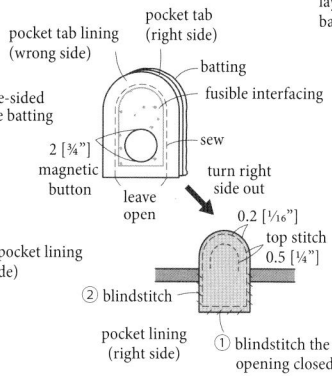

bias binding (wrong side) 0.7 [¼"] ② bias binding

3.5 [1⅜"]

double-sided fusible batting

① machine quilt

bag back pocket (right side)

bag back pocket lining (wrong side)

pocket tab lining (wrong side)

pocket tab (right side)

batting

fusible interfacing

2 [¾"] magnetic button

sew

leave open

turn right side out

0.2 [¹⁄₁₆"]

top stitch 0.5 [¼"]

② blindstitch

pocket lining (right side)

① blindstitch the opening closed

lay the pocket on top of the bag back; baste around the edges

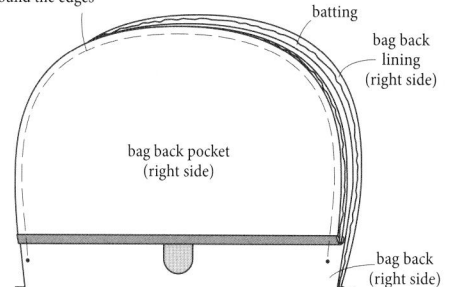

batting

bag back lining (right side)

bag back pocket (right side)

bag back (right side)

1 [⅜"]   top stitch   zipper 25 [9¾"]   batting

bag front (right side)

sew the darts down

bag front lining (wrong side)

flip the zipper right side out; blindstitch the zipper tape to the lining

sew

zipper (wrong side)

bag front (right side)

Gusset

sew the bias binding strips to the right side of the gusset

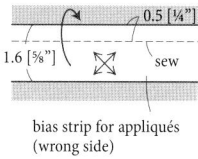

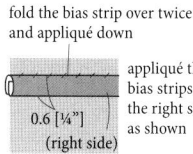

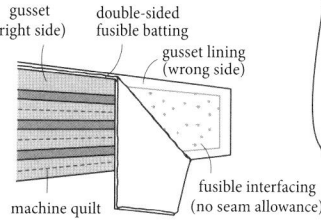

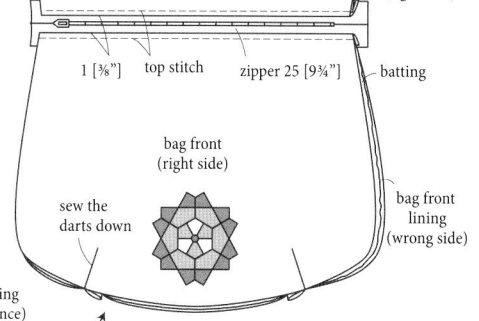

0.5 [¼"]

1.6 [⅝"]   sew

bias strip for appliqués (wrong side)

fold the bias strip over twice and appliqué down

0.6 [¼"] (right side)

appliqué three bias strips to the right side as shown

gusset (right side)

double-sided fusible batting

gusset lining (wrong side)

machine quilt

fusible interfacing (no seam allowance)

Sewing the Bag Together

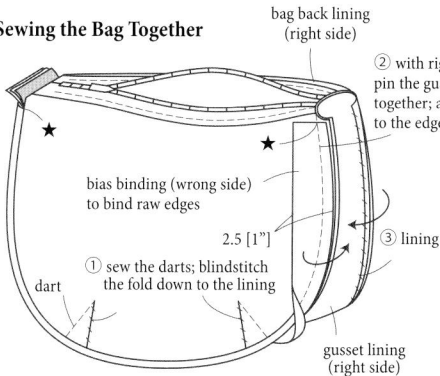

bag back lining (right side)

② with right sides together, pin the gusset and pouch body together; align the bias binding to the edges; sew around all sides

bias binding (wrong side) to bind raw edges

2.5 [1"]

① sew the darts; blindstitch the fold down to the lining

dart

③ lining

gusset lining (right side)

Sewing the Gusset Ends

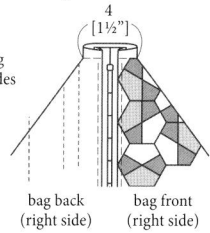

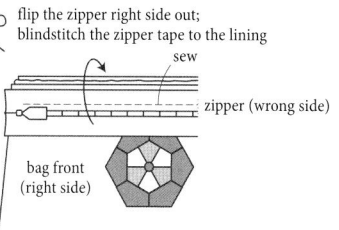

4 [1½"]

bag back (right side)   bag front (right side)

Making the Strap Tabs

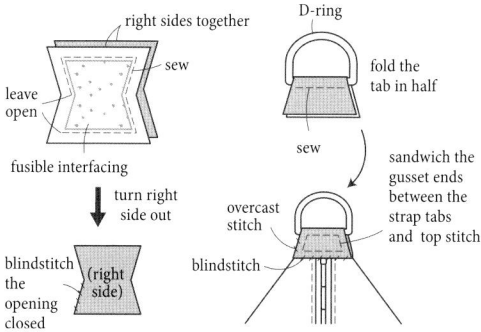

right sides together

sew

leave open

fusible interfacing

turn right side out

blindstitch the opening closed

(right side)

D-ring

fold the tab in half

sew

overcast stitch

blindstitch

sandwich the gusset ends between the strap tabs and top stitch

Zipper Pull

sew

fold

right sides together

5 [2"]

0.5 [¼"]

turn right side out

sew the ends

jump ring

zipper clasp

wooden bead

sew the bead to the fabric tube

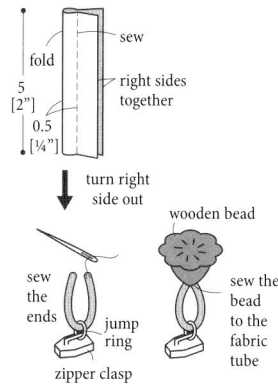

Completed Bag

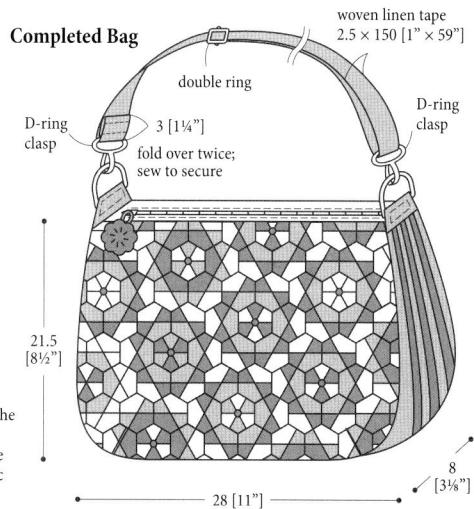

woven linen tape 2.5 × 150 [1" × 59"]

double ring

D-ring clasp

D-ring clasp

3 [1¼"]

fold over twice; sew to secure

21.5 [8½"]

28 [11"]

8 [3⅛"]

shown on p. 40 ## 20 Birdhouses in a Tree Handbag

The template/pattern can be found on Side D of the pattern sheet inserts.

Materials

Assorted fat quarters or scraps (piecing and appliqué)
Beige print (bag front, pocket) - 35 × 70 cm
[13¾" × 27½"]
Beige print (gusset) - 25 × 80 cm [9¾" × 31½"]
Beige check homespun (bag back) - 35 × 35 cm
[13¾" × 13¾"]
Beige plaid homespun (bag opening inner facing)
- 3 × 60 cm [1¼" × 23⅝"]
Beige plaid (lining) - 80 × 75 cm [31½" × 29½"]
Batting - 80 × 75 cm [31½" × 29½"]
Beige plaid (bias binding for pocket) - 3.5 × 30 cm
[1⅜" × 11¾"]
Homespun (bias binding for bag opening) - 2.5 × 60 cm
[1" × 23⅝"]
Fusible interfacing - 80 × 45 cm [31½" × 17¾"]
Woven cotton tape (handles)
bottom layer - 3 × 64 cm [1¼" × 25⅛"]
top layer - 2.2 × 64 cm [⅞" × 25⅛"]
Magnetic Button - 1.6 cm [⅝"] 1 pair
Embroidery floss - colors to match

Directions

1 Cut out the pattern pieces including the lining, facing, batting and fusible interfacing if called for.
2 Appliqué, piece and embroider the design to the bag front and pocket. With wrong sides together, layer the bag front and bag front lining with batting in between. Baste; quilt. Repeat for the pocket. Repeat for the bag back and gusset, but fuse the interfacing to the linings beforehand.
3 Bind the top edge of the pocket. Lay it on top of the bag back aligning edges; baste.
4 With right sides together, pin the gusset to the bag front and bag back; sew. Trim the seam allowances except for the gusset lining. Use the lining to bind the seam allowances and blindstitch down.
5 With right sides together, sew the ends of the bag opening outer facing together to the side of the bag opening. With right sides together, pin to the top edge of the bag opening; sew. Turn right side up and press (the raw edge will be at the top of the bag).
6 Pin the handles in position on the bag opening outer facing. Align and pin the bias binding on top of the bag opening outer facing, sandwiching the handles; sew.
7 Turn the bias binding to the inside on the seam with the handles up. Turn the bias binding seam allowance under on the lining side; blindstitch down to the lining. Top stitch through the middle of the facing/bias binding.
8 Sew the fabric-covered magnetic buttons in place to the bag back and the pocket to finish.

Dimensional Diagram

Bag Front

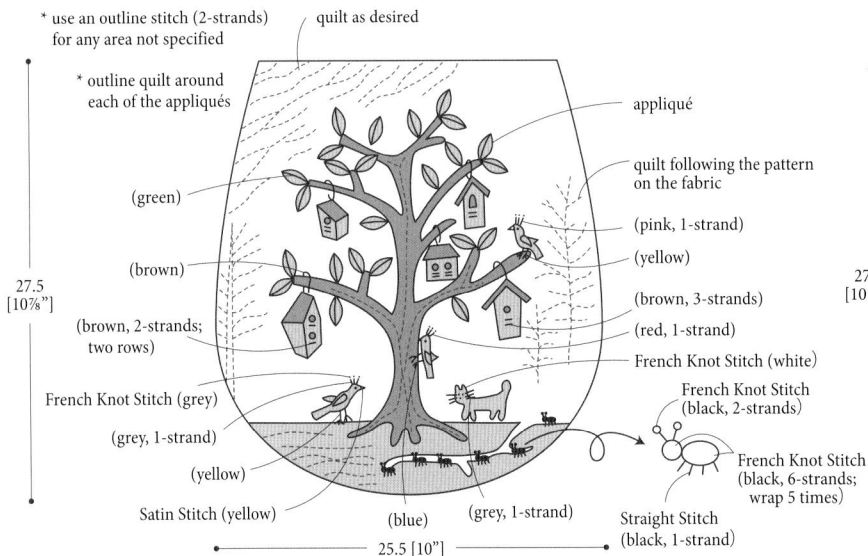

* use an outline stitch (2-strands) for any area not specified

* outline quilt around each of the appliqués

quilt as desired

appliqué

quilt following the pattern on the fabric

(green)

(brown)

(pink, 1-strand)

(yellow)

(brown, 2-strands; two rows)

(brown, 3-strands)

(red, 1-strand)

French Knot Stitch (white)

French Knot Stitch (grey)

French Knot Stitch (black, 2-strands)

(grey, 1-strand)

(yellow)

French Knot Stitch (black, 6-strands; wrap 5 times)

Satin Stitch (yellow)

(blue)

(grey, 1-strand)

Straight Stitch (black, 1-strand)

27.5 [10⅞"]

25.5 [10"]

Bag Back

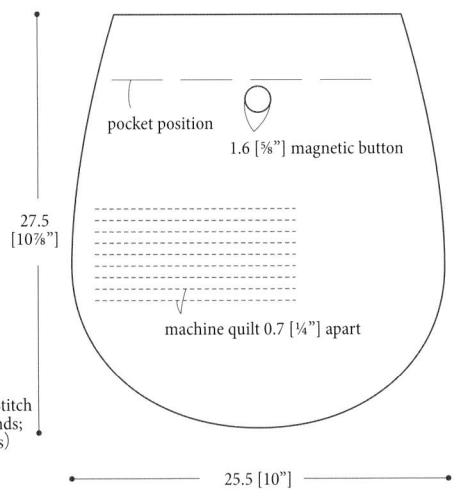

pocket position

1.6 [⅝"] magnetic button

machine quilt 0.7 [¼"] apart

27.5 [10⅞"]

25.5 [10"]

Gusset

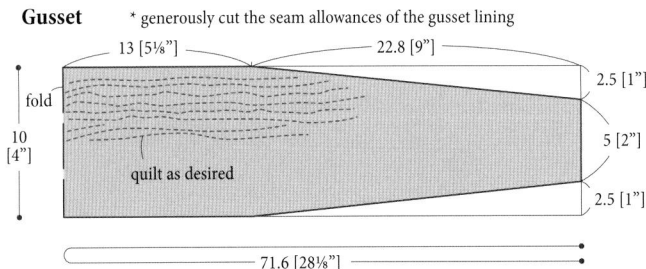

* generously cut the seam allowances of the gusset lining

13 [5⅛"]

22.8 [9"]

2.5 [1"]

fold

5 [2"]

10 [4"]

quilt as desired

2.5 [1"]

71.6 [28⅛"]

Bag Opening Outer Facing

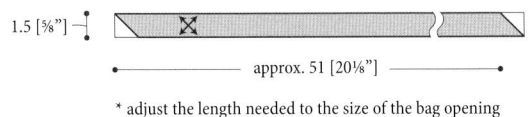

1.5 [⅝"]

approx. 51 [20⅛"]

* adjust the length needed to the size of the bag opening

Pocket

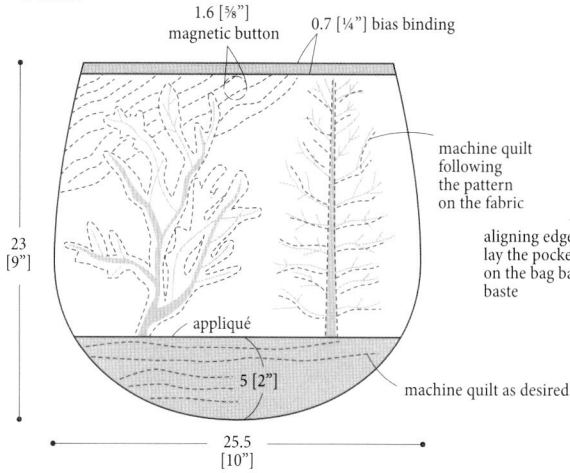

23 [9"]

5 [2"]

25.5 [10"]

1.6 [⅝"] magnetic button

0.7 [¼"] bias binding

machine quilt following the pattern on the fabric

aligning edges lay the pocket on the bag back; baste

appliqué

machine quilt as desired

Bag Back

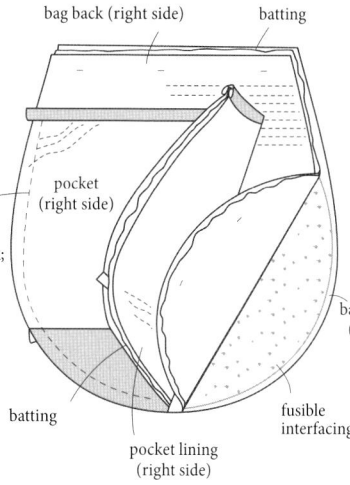

bag back (right side)

batting

pocket (right side)

bag back lining (wrong side)

batting

fusible interfacing

pocket lining (right side)

Magnetic Button (make 2)

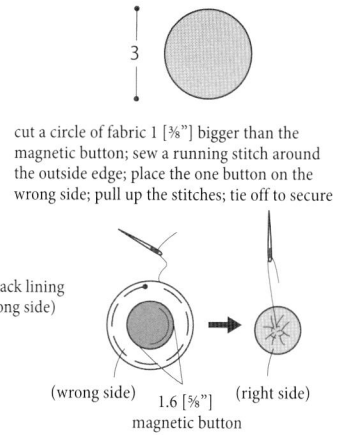

3

cut a circle of fabric 1 [⅜"] bigger than the magnetic button; sew a running stitch around the outside edge; place the one button on the wrong side; pull up the stitches; tie off to secure

(wrong side)

1.6 [⅝"] magnetic button

(right side)

PROJECTS

Gusset

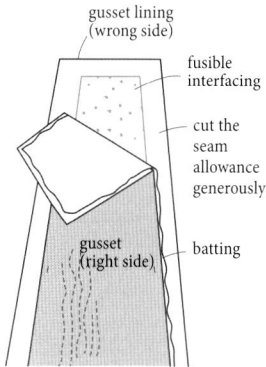

gusset lining (wrong side)

fusible interfacing

cut the seam allowance generously

gusset (right side)

batting

Sewing the Bag Together

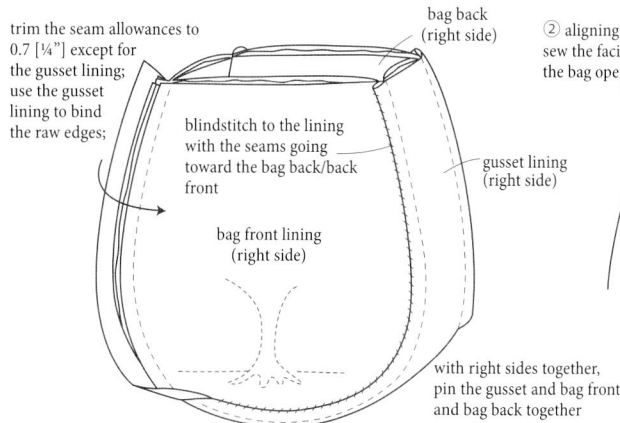

trim the seam allowances to 0.7 [¼"] except for the gusset lining; use the gusset lining to bind the raw edges;

blindstitch to the lining with the seams going toward the bag back/back front

bag front lining (right side)

bag back (right side)

gusset lining (right side)

with right sides together, pin the gusset and bag front and bag back together

Sewing the Facing to the Bag Opening

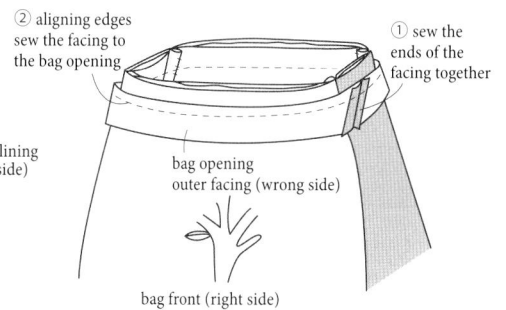

② aligning edges sew the facing to the bag opening

① sew the ends of the facing together

bag opening outer facing (wrong side)

bag front (right side)

Making the Handles

lay the narrower tape on top of the wider tape; top stitch

woven cotton tape for bottom layer of handle 3 [1¼"]

30 [11¾"]

3 [1¼"]

28 [11"]

woven cotton tape for top layer 2.2 [⅞"]

the ends will get sewn within the bag opening

Sewing the Handles to the Bag

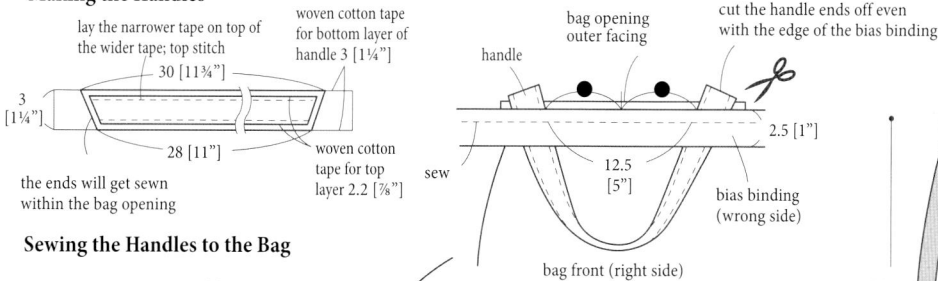

bag opening outer facing

handle

cut the handle ends off even with the edge of the bias binding

2.5 [1"]

12.5 [5"]

bias binding (wrong side)

bag front (right side)

sew

bias binding (right side)

handle

2.5 [1"]

turn under on the seam with the handles up

1.5 [⅝"]

bag front (right side)

bag opening outer facing

turn under the bias binding seam allowance; top stitch through all layers

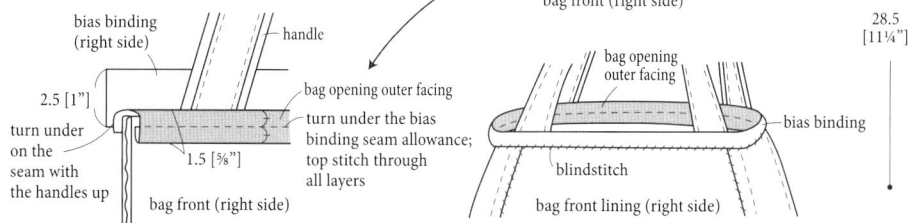

bag opening outer facing

blindstitch

bag front lining (right side)

bias binding

Completed Bag

28.5 [11¼"]

25.5 [10"]

10 [4"]

109

21 Orange Peel Grommet Handbag

The template/pattern can be found on Side D of the pattern sheet inserts.

Materials

Assorted fat quarters or scraps (piecing and appliqué for bag body)
Black plaid homespun (bag body) - 110 × 40 cm [43¼" × 15¾"]
Dk brown homespun (gusset, bag bottom) - 60 × 30 cm [23⅝" × 11¾"]
Homespun (lining) - 100 × 60 cm [39⅜" × 23⅝"]
Batting - 50 × 80 cm [19¾" × 31½"]
Dk brown homespun (bias binding) - 3.5 × 160 cm [1⅜" × 63"]
Heavyweight fusible interfacing (bottom) - 25 × 10 cm [9¾" × 4"]
Fusible interfacing - 70 × 20 cm [27½" × 7⅞"]
Double-sided fusible interfacing - 20 × 20 cm [7⅞" × 7⅞"]
Grommets - 5 cm [2"] 4 pair
Magnetic Button - 2 cm [¾"] 1 pair
Woven cotton tape (handles) - 3 × 96 cm [1¼" × 37¾"]

Directions

1 Cut out the pattern pieces including the lining, facing, batting and fusible interfacing if called for.
2 Piece and appliqué the design to make two of the bag bodies. With wrong sides together, lay the bag body and bag body lining with batting in between. Baste; quilt.
3 Fuse the interfacing to the wrong side of the facings; sew a magnetic button in position to one of them. Align the wrong side of the facing to the right side of the bag body lining; baste around the top edges; blindstitch the bottom edge to the lining. Repeat for the other side.
4 Fuse the double-sided interfacing to the wrong side of the gusset lining. With right sides together, sew the top edge. Turn right side out; make pintucks down the length of the gusset. Make two.
5 With wrong sides together, sew the bag body pieces and the gusset together. Use the bias binding to bind each side of the bag.
6 At the bottom of each gusset, butt the two bias-bound edges together along with the pleats on either side and sew across them to secure.
7 Fuse the interfacing to the wrong side of the bag bottom facing and the bag bottom lining. With wrong sides together, layer the bag bottom and bag bottom facing with batting in between; baste; machine quilt.
8 With right sides together, sew the bag bottom to the bag body, with facing side out. Lay the bag bottom lining over the facing covering the bag bottom seams; blindstitch down.
9 Following the diagrams, open the holes for the grommets in the bag fabric; set the grommets following the manufacturer's directions.
10 Make the tab with the remaining magnetic button sewn in; sew to the bag body lining on the opposite side of the facing with the button.
11 Make the handles; slide them through the grommets and blindstitch them to secure to complete the bag.

Dimensional Diagram

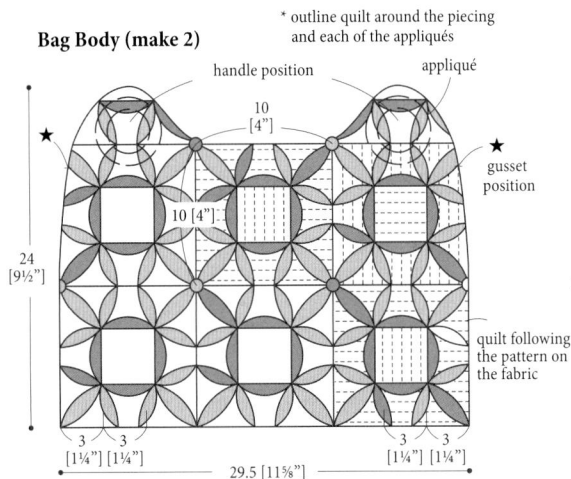

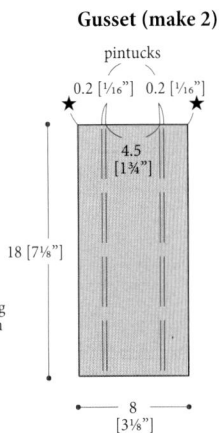

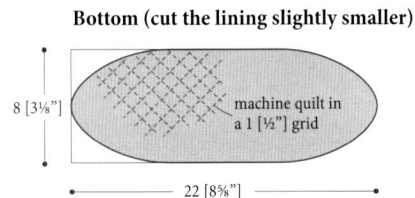

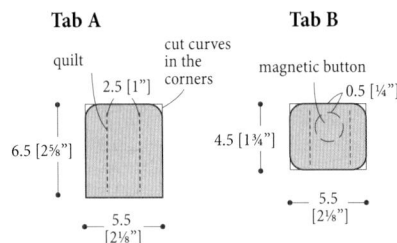

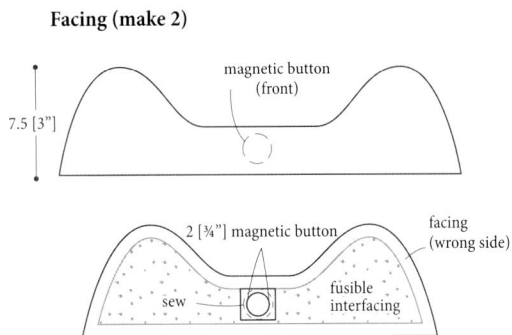

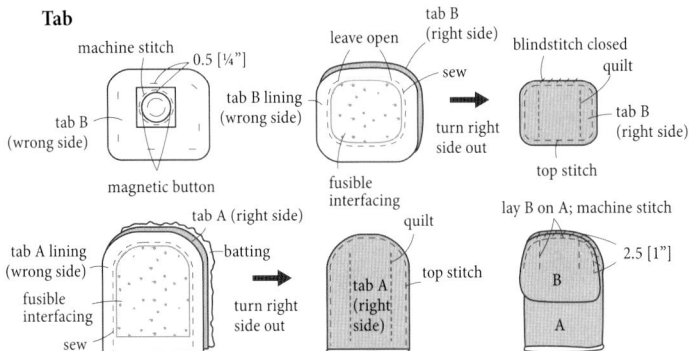

Bag Body (make 2)

* outline quilt around the piecing and each of the appliqués

handle position
appliqué
gusset position
10 [4"]
10 [4"]
24 [9½"]
quilt following the pattern on the fabric
3 [1¼"] 3 [1¼"]
3 [1¼"] 3 [1¼"]
29.5 [11⅝"]

Gusset (make 2)

pintucks
0.2 [1/16"] 0.2 [1/16"]
4.5 [1¾"]
18 [7⅛"]
8 [3⅛"]

Bottom (cut the lining slightly smaller)

machine quilt in a 1 [½"] grid
8 [3⅛"]
22 [8⅝"]

Tab A

quilt
cut curves in the corners
2.5 [1"]
6.5 [2⅝"]
5.5 [2⅛"]

Tab B

magnetic button
0.5 [¼"]
4.5 [1¾"]
5.5 [2⅛"]

Facing (make 2)

magnetic button (front)
7.5 [3"]
2 [¾"] magnetic button
facing (wrong side)
sew
fusible interfacing

Tab

machine stitch
0.5 [¼"]
tab B (wrong side)
magnetic button
leave open
tab B (right side)
sew
tab B lining (wrong side)
fusible interfacing
turn right side out
blindstitch closed
quilt
tab B (right side)
top stitch

tab A lining (wrong side)
fusible interfacing
sew
batting
tab A (right side)
turn right side out
tab A (right side)
top stitch
quilt
lay B on A; machine stitch
2.5 [1"]
B
A

Bag Body

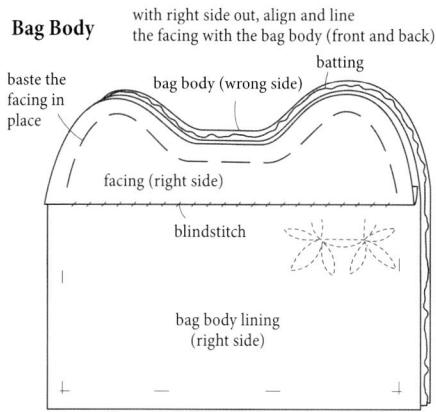

baste the facing in place

with right side out, align and line the facing with the bag body (front and back)

batting

bag body (wrong side)

facing (right side)

blindstitch

bag body lining (right side)

Gusset

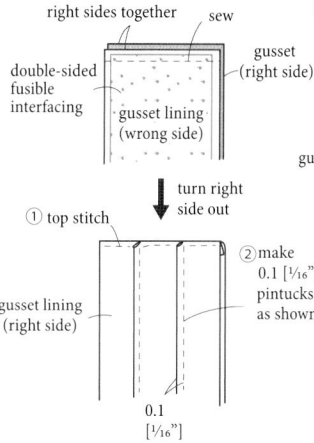

right sides together

sew

double-sided fusible interfacing

gusset (right side)

gusset lining (wrong side)

turn right side out

① top stitch

gusset lining (right side)

② make 0.1 [1/16"] pintucks as shown

0.1 [1/16"]

Sewing the Bag Together

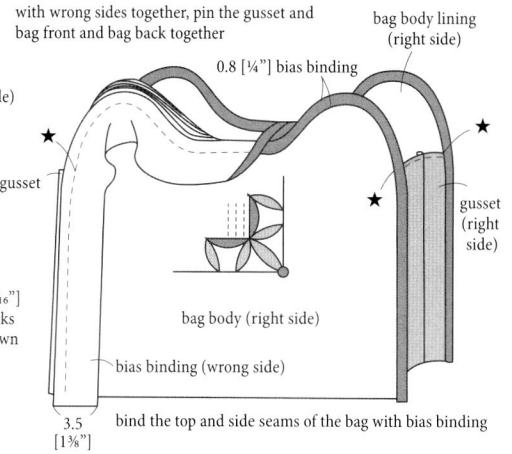

with wrong sides together, pin the gusset and bag front and bag back together

bag body lining (right side)

0.8 [1/4"] bias binding

gusset

★

gusset (right side)

bag body (right side)

bias binding (wrong side)

3.5 [1⅜"]

bind the top and side seams of the bag with bias binding

Pleating the Lower Gussets

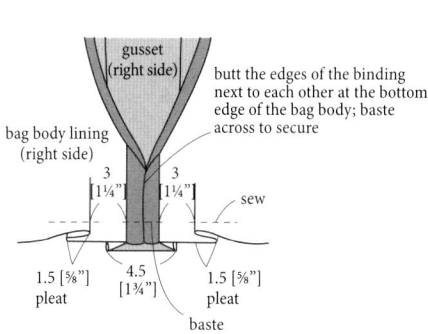

gusset (right side)

bag body lining (right side)

3 [1¼"] 3 [1¼"]

sew

1.5 [⅝"] pleat

4.5 [1¾"]

1.5 [⅝"] pleat

baste

butt the edges of the binding next to each other at the bottom edge of the bag body; baste across to secure

Making the Bag Bottom

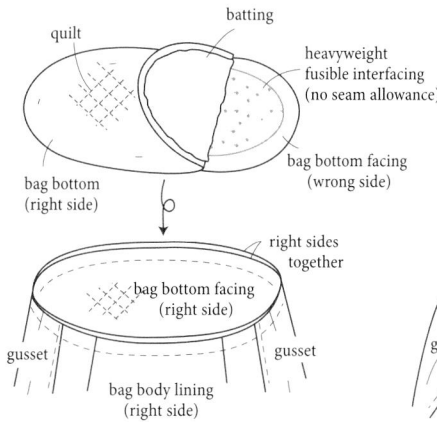

quilt

batting

heavyweight fusible interfacing (no seam allowance)

bag bottom (right side)

bag bottom facing (wrong side)

right sides together

bag bottom facing (right side)

gusset

gusset

bag body lining (right side)

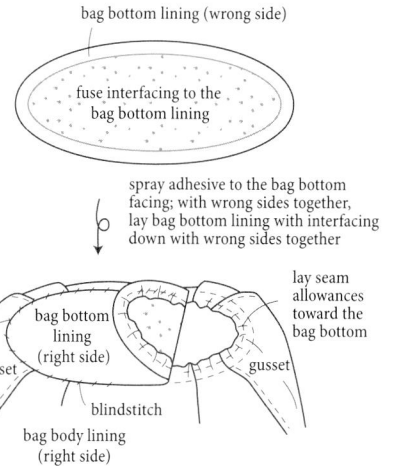

bag bottom lining (wrong side)

fuse interfacing to the bag bottom lining

spray adhesive to the bag bottom facing; with wrong sides together, lay bag bottom lining with interfacing down with wrong sides together

bag bottom lining (right side)

gusset

gusset

blindstitch

lay seam allowances toward the bag bottom

bag body lining (right side)

Making the Handles (make 2)

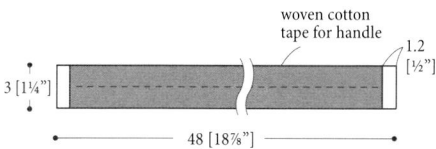

woven cotton tape for handle

1.2 [½"]

3 [1¼"]

48 [18⅞"]

Opening the Grommet Holes

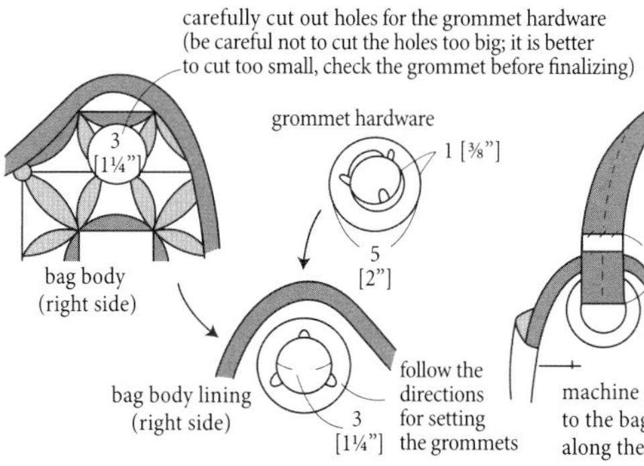

carefully cut out holes for the grommet hardware (be careful not to cut the holes too big; it is better to cut too small, check the grommet before finalizing)

3 [1¼"]

bag body (right side)

grommet hardware

1 [⅜"]

5 [2"]

bag body lining (right side)

follow the directions for setting the grommets

3 [1¼"]

Finishing the Tab and Handle Ends

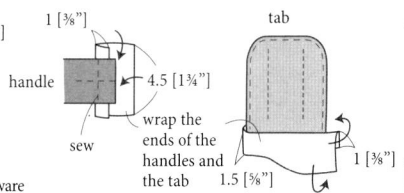

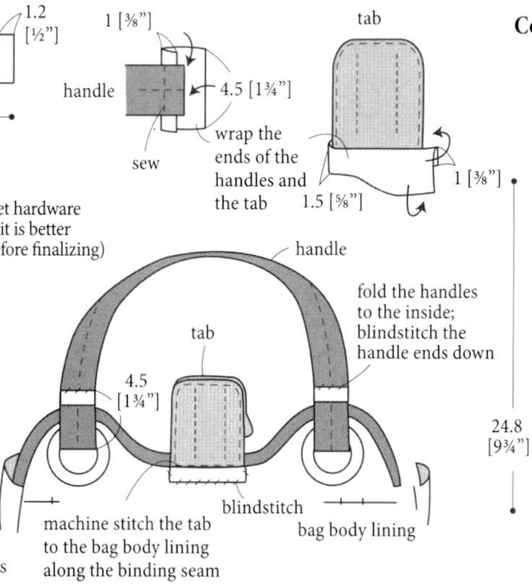

1 [⅜"]

handle

sew

4.5 [1¾"]

tab

wrap the ends of the handles and the tab

1.5 [⅝"]

1 [⅜"]

handle

tab

4.5 [1¾"]

machine stitch the tab to the bag body lining along the binding seam

blindstitch

bag body lining

fold the handles to the inside; blindstitch the handle ends down

Completed Bag

24.8 [9¾"]

31.1 [12¼"]

8 [3⅛"]

Yoko Saito

Originally from Ichikawa City in Chiba Prefecture in Japan, Yoko Saito established her quilting school and shop, Quilt Party, in 1985. She soon garnered a reputation for her masterful use and personal style of "taupe colors," as well as her beautifully precise needlework. In addition to her regular appearances on Japanese television and in magazines, she has published numerous books. In recent years, she has begun to branch out internationally, holding quilt exhibitions and workshops in countries as far as France, Italy and Taiwan. In 2008 she commemorated 30 years of her creative career with the Yoko Saito Quilt Exhibition at the Matsuya department store in Ginza, Tokyo.

Original Title	Saito Yoko no Mainichi Tsukaitai Otona no Bag
Author	Yoko Saito
First Edition	Originally published in Japan in 2012
Copyright	©2012 Yoko Saito, ©2012 Nihon Vogue-Sha; All rights reserved.
Published by:	Nihon Vogue Co., Ltd.
	3-23 Ichigaya Honmura-cho, Shinjuku-ku,
	Tokyo, Japan 162-8705
	http://book.nihonvogue.co.jp
Translation	©2014 Stitch Publications, LLC
English Translation Rights	arranged with Stitch Publications, LLC
	through Tuttle-Mori Agency, Inc.
Published by:	Stitch Publications, LLC
	P.O. Box 16694
	Seattle, WA 98116
	http://www.stitchpublications.com
Printed & Bound	KHL Printing, Singapore
ISBN	978-0-9859746-6-4
PCN	Library of Congress Control Number: 2014930191

Staff

Book Design/Layout	Wakana Takemori
Photography	Toshikatsu Watanabe
	Satoru Suyama
Styling	Reiko Okamoto
Illustrations	Factory Water
Pattern Illustrations	Noriko Hachimonji
Editorial Assistant	Sakae Suzuki
Editor	Nobuko Terashima
Director	Hiroko Kon

Quilt Party, Co., Ltd. (shop and school)

Quilt Party Co., Ltd.
Active Ichikawa 2F
1-23-2, Ichikawa, Ichikawa-shi,
Chiba-Ken, Japan 272-0034

http://www.quilt.co.jp (Japanese)
http://shop.quilt.co.jp/en/index.htm (English)

Creative Staff
Satomi Funamoto
Kazuko Yamada
Katsumi Mizusawa
Terumi Ishida

Photography Collaboration

Photography Studio: Barbie Bleau
Yoyogi, Shibuya-ku, Tokyo Kamizono-cho 3-43 2F
TEL 03-3465-1088 FAX 03-3465-1077
http://www.barbie-bleau.com/index.php

This English edition is published by arrangement with Nihon Vogue Co., Ltd. in care of Tuttle-Mori Agency, Inc., Tokyo

All rights reserved. No part of this publication may be reproduced or transmitted in any form or by any means, electronic or mechanical, including photocopy, recording, or any other information storage or retrieval systems, without written permission of the publisher. The written instructions, photographs, designs and patterns are intended for personal, non-commercial use of the retail purchaser and protected under federal copyright laws.

The original author, publisher and U.S.-based publisher, Stitch Publications, LLC, which has translated and compiled this material, has tried to make all of the contents as accurate as possible, and as such, no warranty is provided nor are results guaranteed. Neither the author, the original publisher, nor Stitch Publications, LLC, assumes any responsibility for any damages or losses incurred that result directly or indirectly from the information presented in this book.